THE WALKER SOCIAL SKILLS CURRICULUM:

THE ACCEPTS PROGRAM

By
Hill M. Walker, Scott McConnell, Deborah Holmes,
Bonnie Todis, Jackie Walker, and Nancy Golden

8700 Shoal Creek Boulevard
Austin, Texas 78757

Copyright © 1988 by Hill Walker, Bonnie Todis, Deborah Holmes, and Gary Horton

All rights reserved. No part of this book
may be reproduced in any form or by any means
without the prior written permission of the publisher.

Printed in the United States of America

8700 Shoal Creek Boulevard
Austin, Texas 78757

13 14 15   04 03 02 01 00

DEDICATION
(From the Senior Author)

To Spicer Dicer
Tireless Writing Companion and Loyal Friend
For All the Lovely Memories

TABLE OF CONTENTS

INTRODUCTION v

SECTION I: CONTEXTUAL AND BACKGROUND INFORMATION RELATING TO THE
ACCEPTS CURRICULUM AND SOCIAL TRAINING 1
    Social Skills Defined 1
    The Importance of Teaching Social Skills 2
    Social Skills and the Mainstreaming Process 3
    Effectiveness of Social Skills Training 4
    Goals and Objectives of the ACCEPTS Curriculum 5
    Evaluation and Revision of the ACCEPTS Curriculum 5
    Consumer Satisfaction Information From Program Users 7
    Overview of the ACCEPTS Program 8

SECTION II: SELECTING TARGET CHILDREN FOR THE ACCEPTS PROGRAM 11
    Measurement Instruments 11
    Screening Procedures 12
    Selection Criteria 12

SECTION III: SERVICE DELIVERY OPTIONS AND STAFF TRAINING 15
    Service Delivery Options 15
    Staff Training Procedures 16

SECTION IV: GUIDELINES FOR TEACHING THE ACCEPTS CURRICULUM 19
    The ACCEPTS Placement Test 19
    The ACCEPTS Reference List 20
    The ACCEPTS Instructional Sequence 20
    The ACCEPTS Teaching Scripts 21
    Teaching Script Example 22
    The ACCEPTS Review Scripts 25
    Review Script Example 25
    The ACCEPTS Correction Procedure 26
    ACCEPTS Behavior Management 29
    Review 32

SECTION V: THE ACCEPTS TEACHING SCRIPTS 33
    (See Appendix 2, page 121-122, for a table of contents of the Teaching Scripts)

SECTION VI: BEHAVIOR MANAGEMENT PROCEDURES 103
    The Classroom Behavior Management System 104
    The Playground Behavior Management System 106
    Procedures for Extending the Program to Other Classroom and Playground Periods 110

REFERENCES 115

APPENDICES 118

INTRODUCTION

The *ACCEPTS* (*A* *C*urriculum for *C*hildren's *E*ffective *P*eer and *T*eacher *S*kills) *Social Skills Curriculum* is designed to teach critically important teacher and peer-to-peer social-behavioral competencies essential for a successful adjustment to the behavioral demands of mainstream settings. The original prototype version of the curriculum was developed as part of a three year *Handicapped Children's Model Program* (HCMP) grant from the U.S. Office of Special Education Programs that focused on the placement and integration components of P.L. 94-142. An overview of this project is contained in Appendix 1. The major goal of the ACCEPTS curriculum is to prepare handicapped children to enter and perform satisfactorily within less restrictive settings. A secondary goal is to directly teach skills that facilitate classroom adjustment and contribute to peer acceptance.

ACCEPTS is designed for use with mildly and moderately handicapped children in the primary and intermediate grades. Teachers in special education and regular classroom settings are viewed as the primary consumers of the curriculum. However, it can be used effectively by other school professionals concerned with either the mainstreaming process or with teaching social-behavioral competencies to children deficient in them—whether handicapped or not. These individuals would include mental health personnel, school counselors, psychologists, social workers, and speech-language therapists.

The ACCEPTS curriculum uses a direct instructional and competency based approach to teaching social skills. It adapts instructional formats for the teaching of social rather than academic content. Twenty-eight skills grouped into five major content areas are taught by the curriculum. The areas are: (1) Classroom Skills, (2) Basic Interaction Skills, (3) Getting Along, (4) Making Friends, and (5) Coping Skills. The *Classroom Skills* area includes behavioral competencies essential for a successful classroom adjustment, e.g., meeting the teacher's expectations. The other four content areas teach skills that determine interactive competence and affect the quality of the child's social adjustment with peers.

THE ACCEPTS curriculum contains the following elements:
— A Placement Test
— A nine-step instructional procedure based on principles of direct instruction
— Guidelines for teaching the curriculum
— Scripts for teaching four critically important teacher-child behavioral competencies and twenty-four peer-to-peer social skills.
— Videotaped examples and nonexamples of the skills to be taught.
— Role play activities and tests to determine skill mastery.
— Activities and formats for use in one-to-one, small group, large group, and entire class teaching situations.
— Behavior management procedures for use during the teaching process and for strengthening correct applications of the skills in classroom and playground settings.

Principles of direct instruction incorporated into the ACCEPTS curriculum include (1) clear definitions and specifications of each skill to be taught, (2) selection and presentation of both instances and noninstances of the correct application/demonstration of each skill, (3) sequencing of skills so that increasing complexity is built into the target child's behavioral repertoire as instruction progresses, (4) provision of a variety of practice activities to build in conceptual and behavioral mastery of each skill, and (5) use of systematic correction procedures that move the target child toward skill mastery.

As noted, social skills are taught using procedures identical to those appropriate for teaching any other subject matter content. Milburn and Cartledge (1981) list five steps for teaching social skills as an academic content area. These are:
(1) Define the behaviors to be taught.
(2) Assess the student's proficiency on them.
(3) Teach the needed skills through presentation of examples requiring responses and providing feedback.
(4) Evaluate the results of teaching and reteach where necessary.
(5) Provide opportunities for practice, generalization and maintenance over time.

In addition, they suggest that social skills training is most effective when it is directed at the child's level of understanding, concerns social skills and behaviors that are relevant and meaningful to her/him, and is conveyed in ways that create interest and motivation. Attempts were made to incorporate all of these steps and guidelines into the teaching procedures for the ACCEPTS curriculum.

The authors believe the ACCEPTS curriculum is an effective means of teaching both handicapped and nonhandicapped children important social-behavioral competencies. The program requires extra time and effort on the part of school personnel for instruction and implementation. However, it is highly effective and fits into regular school schedules well. In fact, the curriculum can be offered as an integral part of the daily academic program for all students enrolled in either special education or regular classroom settings. If implemented correctly, ACCEPTS can have a significant impact upon the adjustment capability and school success of a broad range of elementary school age children.

To benefit from the ACCEPTS curriculum's content and instructional procedures, handicapped children should have the following characteristics: (1) a capacity to imitate and acquire skills through behavioral rehearsal procedures, (2) an ability to listen to instructions and follow directions, (3) rudimentary language skills, and (4) a minimal repertoire of attending behavior. As a general rule, these prerequisites would exclude severely handicapped children. The instructional procedures would have to be revised extensively for effective use with this population. Although children with behavior disorders are often viewed as the handicapped population most in need of social skills training, the ACCEPTS curriculum was designed for use with a broad range of handicapping conditions. The curriculum and instructional procedures may require special adaptations when used with certain categories of disability, e.g., hearing or visually impaired children, orthopedically involved, and so forth.

Depending upon the target child's rate of progress, five to ten weeks of daily instruction will be required to move a handicapped child through the curriculum. Less instructional time will be required for nonhandicapped children. One ACCEPTS skill should be taught and mastered daily, if possible, with approximately 40 to 45 minutes devoted to each instructional session. As already noted, the ACCEPTS curriculum should be taught as an academic content area similar to reading, math, or language arts. The curriculum content can be taught using a variety of instructional formats, including one-to-one, small group, large group, or the entire class. Instruction can occur either in the classroom context or in a secluded area outside the classroom, depending upon the teacher's preference.

Research on social skills training suggests that small group teaching formats are most effective for teaching social behavior content (La Greca & Santogrossi, 1980). A small group format involving the target handicapped child and several nonhandicapped peers (if possible) is recommended by the authors.

The material is divided into six major sections: (I) Contextual and Background Information Relating to the ACCEPTS Curriculum and Social Skills Training Procedures, (II) Criteria and Procedures for Screening, Identifying, and Selecting Target Children, (III) Service Delivery Options and Staff Training, (IV) Guidelines for Teaching the ACCEPTS Curriculum, (V) Teaching Scripts and Instructional Procedures, and (VI) Behavior Management Procedures for Strengthening Application of the Skills in Classroom and Playground Settings. The reader is urged to become familiar with all of the material herein before beginning the teaching process.

SECTION I
CONTEXTUAL AND BACKGROUND INFORMATION RELATING TO THE ACCEPTS CURRICULUM AND SOCIAL SKILLS TRAINING

The purpose of this section is to provide background information on the ACCEPTS curriculum, social skills training procedures, and their importance to both the development and adjustment of handicapped children and the mainstreaming process. The following topics will be dealt with in this section: (1) Social skills defined, (2) The importance of teaching social skills, (3) Social skills and the mainstreaming process, (4) Effectiveness of social skills training, (5) Goals and objectives of the ACCEPTS curriculum, (6) Evaluation and revision of the curriculum, (7) Consumer satisfaction information from program users, and (8) An overview of the ACCEPTS Program.

Social Skills Defined

Definitions of social skills range from tactics of social influence to interpersonal skills that determine social competence (see reviews by Gresham, 1981; Michelson and Wood, 1980; Van Hasselt, Hersen, Whitehill and Bellack, 1979; Hops, in press). Social skills as defined by the present authors and taught by the curriculum have three elements. These are social responses and skills that:
(1) Allow one to initiate and maintain positive relationships with others,
(2) Contribute to peer acceptance and to a successful classroom adjustment, and
(3) Allow one to cope effectively and adaptively with the social environment.

The ACCEPTS curriculum teaches two major types of social skills: (1) Critical classroom behaviors that contribute to a successful classroom adjustment as defined by teachers, e.g., listening to instructions, following directions, making assistance needs known in an appropriate manner, and (2) Peer-to-peer social skills that contribute to social competence and peer acceptance, e.g., basic interaction skills, conversation skills, knowledge of how to make friends, and so forth.

The authors devoted considerable time, effort, and research attention to selection of the *classroom* and *peer-to-peer skills* included in the ACCEPTS curriculum. As part of the SBS (*Social Behavior Survival*) project's larger focus (See Appendix 1), over 1,500 teachers in the U.S. and Canada responded to a rating instrument that required them to rate the importance of 56 adaptive behaviors in facilitating a successful classroom adjustment. There was broad consensus among and between the teacher groups making up the sample as to the most and least important behavioral competencies. The most consistently high rated items across teachers were incorporated into the ACCEPTS curriculum under the Classroom Skills content area (see Appendix 2 for a listing of the skills and content areas taught by the ACCEPTS curriculum).

The peer-to-peer social skills included were selected using three methods: (1) A review of the existing literature on the identification of key social skills discriminating between socially competent and incompetent children (e.g., Gottman, Gonso and Rasmussen, 1975), (2) A review and analysis of the social skills taught and outcomes achieved within social skills training programs reported in the literature (e.g., La Greca and Santogrossi, 1980), and (3) A logical analysis of the skills and competencies that would be required for handicapped children to cope effectively with the social demands of mainstream settings. The list of social skills also incorporates those behavioral areas and specific skills that have been empirically related to social competence as measured by sociometric tests (Gottman et al., 1975). In the social skills area, these include: *Knowledge of how to make friends, communication skills and distributing and receiving positive social behavior.*

Curricula material and instructional procedures are incorporated into the ACCEPTS curriculum for all of these skills. Attempts were made to select an array of skills that would be functional, relevant, teachable, and of sufficient breadth to impact upon social-behavioral competence.

The Importance of Teaching Social Skills

Social skills have important implications for child development and are a major determinant of social competence. Retrospective and longitudinal studies show that children with limited social competence are at risk for a variety of psychological and related problems. For example, socially isolated, incompetent children are more likely to (a) *develop juvenile delinquency* (Roff, Sells & Golden, 1972), (b) *drop out of school* (Ulmann, 1957), (c) *have bad conduct discharges from the military* (Roff, 1961), and (d) *experience mental health problems in adulthood* (Cowen, Pederson, Babigan, Izzo & Trost, 1973). Conversely, high social status in childhood has been related to superior academic achievement (Laughlin, 1954; Muma, 1965, 1968) and adequate interpersonal adjustment in later life (Barclay, 1966).

These findings were obtained with groups of nonhandicapped individuals. Handicapped children are likely to be *less* socially skilled and competent than nonhandicapped individuals and subject to even greater developmental risks. Many handicapped children are in urgent need of direct instruction in social skills that will improve their social competence and ability to cope effectively with the demands of the social environment.

There is evidence that the importance of child social development and social skills training is being increasingly recognized by the mental health professions, by special educators, and by regular educators. Stephens (1981) suggests that teaching socially desirable behavior will no doubt be the *Zeitgeist* of the next decade, and that the rising tide of published texts concerning theoretical and practical aspects of teaching positive social behavior are salient indications of this professional interest. These outcomes are doubtless a result of a new awareness of the importance of social behavior to a variety of adjustments in vocational, academic, and interpersonal areas and also a recognition of the importance of positive social relationships to the growth of social competence (Asher & Taylor, 1981; Hartup, 1979).

Special issues of major professional journals are being devoted to social skills training and/or the mainstreaming process (e.g., *Teaching Exceptional Children, Analysis and Intervention in Developmental Disabilities, The Directive Teacher*). The field's experience with the mainstreaming process and the problems associated with the effective integration of handicapped children has highlighted the need for systematic social skills training. In a survey of special education teachers relating to the content and organization of an earlier version of the ACCEPTS curriculum, 21 of 23 teachers indicated that the social skills deficits and maladaptive behaviors that many handicapped children display are major barriers to effective mainstreaming.

There has been a growing concern with the social-behavioral status of preschool handicapped children and its relationship to the LRE provision of P.L. 94-142. The U.S. Office of Special Education Programs identified five priority areas for its research institutes in the area of early education of the handicapped. One of them was development of a social skills curriculum to prepare handicapped children for less restrictive environments. Leaders in the field of early childood education have long viewed child social development as an extremely important factor in school adjustment (Guralnick, 1978, 1981; La Greca, 1981).

Only recently have educators begun to realize the extent to which they can positively influence the social competence, adjustment, and acceptance of handicapped children. Systematic social skills training is an extremely effective means of doing so.

Social Skills and the Mainstreaming Process

Handicapped children are required to make two major social-behavioral adjustments upon entering mainstream settings. They must meet the receiving teacher's minimum behavioral standards and expectations with respect to following classroom rules and responding academically. In addition, handicapped children must learn to cope effectively with a new peer group. It is apparent that many mainstreamed handicapped children are severely deficient in their ability to make these adjustments.

It was assumed by the framers and advocates of P.L. 94-142 that teachers in mainstream settings would be able to accommodate handicapped children effectively and that exposure to nonhandicapped peer groups would facilitate the behavioral normalization and social development of mainstreamed children. Neither assumption appears to be borne out by research conducted since passage of the law (see Gresham, 1981, 1982; Gottlieb, 1979).

Many handicapped children are unable to meet the behavioral standards and expectations that teachers in less restrictive settings hold for child behavior. Nevertheless, the implementation of P.L. 94-142 has produced powerful pressures for regular teachers to accommodate handicapped children and to assume responsibility for their education and overall development. Traditionally, regular teachers have developed neither the technical management/instructional skills necessary to accommodate handicapped children, nor assumed any direct responsibility for them. Special educators have assumed this function via a direct service model. Survey research shows that teachers do not feel either competent or comfortable in accommodating such children (MacMillan, Jones & Meyers, 1976; Sarason & Doris, 1978).

Further, Keogh and Levitt (1976) report that regular teachers are quite concerned about having control over who is mainstreamed into their classrooms, their ability to meet the needs of mainstreamed handicapped children, and the availability of support services and technical assistance. These concerns are not surprising. In fact, they are to be expected given the relative isolation of regular teachers from the broad range of handicapped children. These findings suggest that receiving teachers in mainstream settings may view many handicapped children as being inappropriately placed in their classrooms. If so, teachers may behave in ways that would make it a self-fulfilling prophecy! (Brophy & Good, 1970, 1974).

Of equal, and perhaps even greater significance to the development of handicapped children, is their ability to cope with the pressures and demands of the peer groups they encounter within mainstream settings. One of the major assumptions underlying P.L. 94-142 was that through exposure to nonhandicapped peers, mainstreamed handicapped children would develop normal standards and patterns of behavior, would acquire social skills and improve their social competence, and would engage in social participation with nonhandicapped peers. What is the research evidence on this question?

Studies of mainstreamed handicapped children show that they do not automatically imitate the behavior of nonhandicapped peers, nor do they interact with them on any kind of consistent basis (Gresham, 1981, 1982). A number of studies have shown that mainstreamed handicapped children have very infrequent social contact with their nonhandicapped peers—even within freeplay settings where the probability of such contacts is much greater (Bruininks, 1978; Bryan, 1974; Allen, Benning & Drummond, 1972; Feitelson, Weintraub & Michael, 1972, and Ray, 1974). Gresham (1981) makes the point that handicapped children do not vicariously acquire social skills through observation of nonhandicapped peer models unless they are instructed, prompted, trained, or reinforced for doing so. Thus, the assumption that handicapped children will become more socially skilled through simple exposure to nonhandicapped peers appears untenable. Handicapped children must actively, socially participate to acquire social skills and develop social competence. The evidence strongly suggests they do not socially participate in mainstream settings (Gresham, 1982; Gottlieb, 1979).

The available evidence on the social acceptance of mainstreamed handicapped children by their nonhandicapped peers is equally discouraging. Gresham (1981) reviews studies that show lack of peer acceptance for *mentally retarded* (Ballard, Corman, Gottlieb & Kaufman, 1978; Gottlieb, 1975; Bruininks, Rynders & Gross, 1974; Goodman, Gottlieb & Harrison, 1972, and Gottlieb & Budoff, 1973), *learning disabled* (Bruininks, 1978; Bryan, 1974, 1976, 1978; Bryan & Wheeler, 1972, and La Greca & Mesibov, 1979) and *emotionally disturbed* (behavior disordered) children (Cowen, Pederson, Babigan, Izzo & Trost, 1973; Morgan, 1977; Pekarik, Prinz, Liebert, Weintraub & Neale, 1976, and Victor & Halverson, 1976). It is likely that such lack of peer acceptance would be found across the broad range of handicapping conditions.

Teachers in mainstream settings are not trained to view peer-to-peer social skills as important nor as something they should be held accountable for. Since regular and special teachers are not likely to assume the initiative in developing the social competence of handicapped children, and since this goal will not be achieved as a simple artifact of placement within less restrictive settings, it seems imperative that procedures be developed, tested, and validated for preparing handicapped children for the demands, pressures, and realities of mainstream settings. They must also be trained to meet the receiving teacher's minimal behavioral standards. Recent research by Dwiggins (1981) suggests strongly that teachers in mainstream settings do not adjust their standards downward to accommodate the reduced capacities of either severely or mildly handicapped children.

It is the authors' view that handicapped children should be prepared to a much greater extent than they currently are to meet the minimal behavioral demands of mainstream settings. This would take considerable pressure off the receiving teacher and improve the mainstreamed child's chances of surviving effectively within the setting. If this were the case it would be likely that the mainstreaming process would be a more useful and productive experience for everyone concerned—the handicapped child, peers, and receiving teachers.

Effectiveness of Social Skills Training

Social acceptance is a function of four general classes of child characteristics (Foster & Ritchey, 1979): (1) Physical attractiveness, (2) Special skills and competencies, especially athletic skills, (3) academic competence, and (4) a repertoire of social skills. While physical attractiveness, athletic prowess and academic competence are related in some degree to social acceptance, it appears that one's repertoire of social skills is the most important determinant of social acceptance for both handicapped and nonhandicapped children (Michelson & Wood, 1980).

To date, an impressive number of studies on teaching social skills has been reported in the literature (see reviews by Van Hasselt et al., 1979; Michelson & Wood, 1980; Foster & Ritchey, 1979; Gresham, 1981, 1982, and Hops, in press). These studies provide powerful and convergent evidence that systematic social skills training can: (1) Teach social skills that allow children to cope more effectively with their social environments, (2) Increase the number of social contacts with peers, (3) Increase the rate of social interaction during peer contacts, (4) Improve the quality of social behavior during peer exchanges, (5) Improve social competence, and (6) Broaden peer acceptance as measured by sociometric tests or peer nomination devices. The developmental implications of these findings for both handicapped and nonhandicapped children are very significant.

Most of the research conducted to date on social skills training has involved nonhandicapped children. However, a recent review of social skills training with handicapped populations by Gresham (1981) provides impressive evidence that both the social competence and social acceptance of handicapped children can be improved via social skills training. Additional research needs to be conducted with handicapped children in the social skills area that (1) validates the effectiveness of different models of training, (2) demonstrates the training's effectiveness within mainstream settings, (3) impacts on both classroom adjustment and peer-to-peer social competence, and (4) demonstrates persistence within and transfer across different settings within the natural environment. In spite of these limitations, social skills training with both handicapped and nonhandicapped children appears to be highly cost-effective and well worth the time and effort.

Goals and Objectives of the ACCEPTS Curriculum

ACCEPTS is designed to achieve the following outcomes:
(1) To facilitate the social development of handicapped children.
(2) To prepare them to meet the behavioral demands and expectations that exist in less restrictive settings.
(3) To improve the social acceptance of handicapped children by their nonhandicapped peers.

If the ACCEPTS curriculum content is taught according to the guidelines presented in Section IV of this volume, and systematic behavior management procedures are applied within natural settings to strengthen previously taught social skills, it is likely that all three of these outcomes will be achieved with the majority of handicapped children exposed to it. However, it should be noted that even though the curriculum teaches critical classroom behaviors as well as peer-to-peer social skills, it was *not* designed as a behavior management program.

Many children with behavior disorders (aggression, conduct disorders, social withdrawal) can benefit from social skills training. However, for such children, social skills training should be a secondary rather than a primary intervention. Social skills training alone is not sufficiently powerful to remediate conduct disorders, child aggression, or extreme forms of social withdrawal. Powerful behavior change procedures should be implemented initially to achieve this goal, followed by systematic social skills training, if appropriate.

Evaluation and Revision of the ACCEPTS Curriculum

Two formal evaluations of the ACCEPTS curriculum were carried out by the authors during the 1980-81 and 1981-82 school years. Twenty-eight handicapped children enrolled in self-contained settings within the elementary age range participated in study one and an additional twenty participated in study two. Handicapping conditions represented in the two samples included learning disabled, educable mentally retarded, language impaired, emotionally handicapped, multiply handicapped, and neurologically impaired. In both studies, SBS project staff members assumed responsibility for the daily teaching and behavior management of the target children during selected classroom and playground periods.

Study One. In study one, a post only, experimental-control group design was used to assess effects of the social skills training (see Walker, McConnell, Walker, Clarke, Todis, Cohen, & Rankin, in press).

The 28 handicapped children were randomly assigned to one of three groups. These were: (1) Social skills training plus contingency management procedures, (2) Social skills training only, and (3) control. There were ten children in group one, eight in group two, and ten in the control group.

Group one children were taught teacher-child critical classroom behaviors (facilitative of classroom adjustment) and peer-to-peer social skills using the ACCEPTS curriculum and instructional procedures. Behavior management procedures were applied in the classroom and on the playground for group one children to strengthen specific skills taught by the curriculum. Group two children received social skills training only. Control children received no social skills training or behavior management during this study.

Training required four to seven weeks and was conducted using small group teaching formats. Teacher ratings, a criterion role play test (CRP) and behavioral observation data recorded in classroom and playground settings were used to assess changes in child behavior attributable to the intervention procedures.

Results favored the two experimental groups over the control group on all three dependent measures. However, statistically significant differences were obtained only on the criterion role play test and classroom observation data. One of three interactive measures (interactive inappropriate) derived from playground observations approached significance at $p < .06$. No significant differences were obtained between the two experimental groups on any of the measures. However, group one children were favored on teacher ratings of classroom and peer-to-peer skills as well as playground observations.

These initial evaluation results were encouraging, but also suggested areas in which the intervention procedures could be strengthened. The intervention package was revised to improve its teachability, power, and instructional precision. The revision included a more intensive curriculum and the addition of group contingencies to the behavior management system to involve peers more directly in the process of improving the social-behavioral competence of target handicapped children.

Feedback from ACCEPTS trainers and cooperating teachers in this study was extremely valuable in the curriculum revision process. In addition, the authors designed a questionnaire for completion by special education teachers regarding procedures needed to effectively integrate handicapped children into less restrictive settings. The questionnaire contained two sections and was administered to a sample of 24 special education teachers. Section I dealt with the feasibility of the general approach to integration represented by the SBS program. Section II contained a series of questions dealing with preferred characteristics of an instructional package for teaching social skills.

Summary responses of the sample to the questionnaire items are contained in Appendix 3. Section I responses indicated the teachers viewed the SBS approach as a needed and viable one. Information obtained from responses to Section II items was used to redesign the ACCEPTS instructional package and to increase its relevance to the needs, concerns and preferences of special education teachers.

Study Two. This study evaluated effects of the revised and expanded version of the ACCEPTS curriculum. An experimental-control group design was used and 20 handicapped children in grades 2 to 5 were randomly assigned to one of these 2 groups, e.g., 10 experimental and 10 control.

Children in the experimental group received: (1) direct instruction on critical classroom and peer-to-peer social skills, (2) *individual* contingency management procedures to increase the use of critical classroom skills, and (3) coaching and *group* contingency management programming to increase the use of peer-to-peer social skills in playground settings. Teacher ratings and behavioral observations of classroom and peer-to-peer social skills were collected for all children at four time points, e.g., (1) before training, (2) during training, (3) immediately following the end of training, and (4) at two-month followup. In addition, a criterion role play test was completed for all participating children (experimental and control) immediately after training.

As in study one, the results showed significantly higher performance levels for experimental children on the criterion role play test. However, the experimental children's regular teachers did not perceive that there had been significant changes produced in their classroom and playground behavior even though observation data indicated that this was the case. Statistically significant changes were produced for experimental children on three measures derived from direct observations of their behavior in classroom and playground settings. These were: (1) Percent of time spent on task (classroom), (2) Percent of time spent engaged in social participation with peers (playground), and (3) Percent of total interactive behavior having verbal content (playground). Significant changes on these measures did not occur for control children.

Even though powerful changes were produced for experimental children during implementation of the ACCEPTS curriculum and accompanying behavior management procedures, they tended not to maintain at post and followup assessments. This is consistent with a large body of evidence which indicates that short term intervention effects do not produce enduring behavior changes unless systematic maintenance procedures are implemented (See Stokes & Baer, 1977; Walker, 1979). More durable effects can be produced by thoroughly implementing the program over a much longer period of time and by implementing low-cost variations of the procedures on an as needed basis after program completion.

These results are encouraging in that they demonstrate the ACCEPTS program not only teaches social-behavioral social skills effectively as indicated by role play test results, but also produces observable changes in the behavior of handicapped children in both classroom and playground settings. If changes of this nature are maintained over the long term in natural environments, they can powerfully influence the adjustment capability and coping skills of handicapped children.

The ACCEPTS program was independently replicated during the 1981-82 school year within two school districts in the state of Washington. The sites were Bellevue and Issaquah, Washington. The results of both replications are highly encouraging.

In Bellevue, the special education director and a program consultant from a Seattle area Education Service District, with limited technical assistance provided by the ACCEPTS developers, trained and supervised six resource room teachers' teaching-implementation of the program. All of the children involved in the replication had been diagnosed as learning disabled. All teachers involved responded enthusiastically to the program and indicated that they could see significant improvement in the target children's behavior repertoires. Informal observation data collected by the replication coordinators confirmed these teacher observations. However, the data were of an anecdotal, unstandardized nature. The major difficulty reported was resource personnel limitations in implementing daily behavior management procedures in playground settings.

A school psychologist in Issaquah, Washington ran four replication groups through the ACCEPTS curriculum during the spring of 1982. These were (1) five third and fourth grade resource room students, (2) four fifth and sixth grade resource room students, (3) four fifth and sixth grade resource room students with severe communication and social skill deficits, and (4) seven intermediate-aged self-contained students who were classified as severe learning disabled. The ACCEPTS program worked best with groups one, three, and four and was regarded as cost-effective and feasible. The supervising psychologist noted that children tended to learn the social skills in the group instructional situation, but did not naturally generalize them to natural social situations.

It is possible that *nonhandicapped* children would synthesize the skills and incorporate them into their ongoing behavior patterns. However, it is the authors' experience that handicapped children need to be prompted, cued, reinforced, and given feedback in interactive settings in order for the skills to be demonstrated reliably.

The positive outcomes from these replications are gratifying. Further, they suggest the ACCEPTS curriculum is quite usable by school personnel within existing school contexts.

Consumer Satisfaction Information from Program Users

During the 1981-82 school year, the ACCEPTS program developers trained a total of 157 professionals in the curriculum. The training was delivered via one or two-day inservice workshops and occurred in five sites in the states of Oregon and Washington. In every case, the training was initiated by representatives from school districts and education service districts.

The authors developed a consumer satisfaction instrument to query workshop participants and users about the curriculum and the accompanying behavior management procedures. A copy of it is contained in Appendix 4. The form uses a one through seven scale to assess satisfaction, with one being low and seven high. The form also contains six YES/NO questions relating to the ACCEPTS program.

Of the 157 professionals trained, 15 users of the actual program completed this form after the program was terminated. Results of their responses are summarized by item in Appendix 5. These individuals had applied the program to an average of 4.15 handicapped children each.

Inspection of Appendix 5 indicates that the program users were very enthusiastic about the ACCEPTS program. All of the ratings exceeded 6.00 except one that averaged 5.44 (Item 7). Further, they gave the program very high marks in terms of its ability to positively affect the social and educational development of handicapped children.

The remainder of the sample (N = 142) completed the form at the end of workshop training. These individual's professional roles were as administrators, teachers, or consultants. Summary responses for these three groups are presented in Appendix 5 using the same presentation format as for program users.

Individuals in these three groups were equally enthusiastic about the program and the level of their satisfaction approximated that of actual program users. The lowest average satisfaction rating across the three groups was 5.41 (Item 7 for administrators). It is interesting to note the very small standard deviations for all respondent groups. This suggests a high level of positive consensus about the program.

These data suggest that both users and potential users are quite enthusiastic about the ACCEPTS program. The authors regard this kind of information as important, useful, and socially valid (Kazdin, 1977). Further, it is a direct reflection of the professional acceptance of the program and its perceived value.

Overview of the ACCEPTS Program.

The ACCEPTS program was designed as a comprehensive approach to the teaching of social skills to handicapped children. The program contains Identification Procedures to select appropriate candidates, Teaching Guidelines for effective instruction, Scripts and Formats for teaching 28 social skills, and Behavior Management Procedures to strengthen application of the skills in natural settings. Careful attention to each of these program elements is essential to a successful use of the program.

A direct instructional approach was selected for teaching the ACCEPTS curriculum content because a) of its demonstrated success in teaching instructionally naïve students complex academic skills (Carnine & Silbert, 1980) and b) research evidence indicates that handicapped children do not vicariously acquire skills unless they are directly prompted, instructed, or reinforced for doing so (Gresham, 1981). In addition, a series of videotaped vignettes was developed to illustrate differences between correct and incorrect demonstrations- applications of social skills taught by the curriculum. These vignettes are integrated into the ACCEPTS instructional procedures and are an important component of the overall program.

The vignettes were designed to teach standards governing correct and incorrect applications of each skill, illustrate the critical elements of each skill, and communicate information regarding the range of situations in which the skill could be applied. Scenes were developed to accompany 23 of the 28 skills taught by the curriculum. Primary grade level children were recruited to be actresses and actors in the vignettes. Scripts were prepared and the children coached in them to dramatize the skill's application.

These video scenes were incorporated into the instructional procedures for each of the 23 skills. A positive example of the skill being correctly applied is shown first. The next scene presents a different positive example or a negative non-example of the skill in which the model either fails to use the skill or applies it inappropriately. The third scene in the teaching sequence presents still another positive example in which the model correctly and appropriately applies the skill—followed by a positive consequence. Finally, one or more scenes are presented that illustrate a range of situations in which the skill can be used appropriately. Variations in the skill's application that might be necessary are also illustrated in these scenes. Role play activities and instructions are provided for the teacher's use in developing those skills for which video scenes are not available.

These vignettes are contained in the ACCEPTS training tape that accompanies this curriculum. Although the curriculum can be taught successfully without it, it is strongly recommended that the videotape be used in the instructional process whenever possible.

The ACCEPTS program is designed for the broad range of mildly to moderately handicapped children in the K-6 grade level range. Special skills are not required to implement the program other than those involved in teaching. Section III of this volume contains a description of various delivery options you can consider in using the program, as well as staff training procedures. You are urged to study this section carefully before using the program.

SECTION II
SELECTING TARGET CHILDREN FOR THE ACCEPTS PROGRAM

Children who are deficient in either appropriate *classroom behavioral competencies* or peer-to-peer *social skills* are appropriate candidates for the ACCEPTS program. Some children have marked deficits in both these areas, while others are deficient in only one area. A child who exhibits below average performance in one of these areas may often not be deficient in the other, therefore, in the screening-identification process, the behavioral status of referred children should be evaluated in *both* classroom and free play or playground settings.

A combination of teacher and/or playground supervisor ratings, and direct observations in classroom and freeplay settings are used to screen and select children for the ACCEPTS program. School professionals are, of course, free to apply the program to any individuals or groups of children whom they feel are in need of social skills training. The procedures and criteria to be described below are presented for the reader's convenience and discretionary use. They were used by the ACCEPTS developers and will identify children who are in need of social skills training, and who are similar to the population of handicapped children the program was developed for and tested upon. Measurement instruments, screening procedures, and selection criteria are described below.

Measurement Instruments

The ACCEPTS *Screening Checklist* is contained in Appendix 6. This form is divided into two sections that measure, respectively, *classroom behavior* and *peer-to-peer* social behavior. The child's teachers should complete *both* sections of the checklist. In addition, one or more of the child's playground supervisors should complete Section II dealing with peer social behavior.

The ACCEPTS Checklist consists of carefully selected items that (1) measure the quality of the target child's classroom and social behavior, and that (2) contribute directly to the adequacy of her/his adjustments in these two areas. The checklist should be completed by adult supervisors in all settings where the child's behavioral status is considered to be a problem.

A direct observational measure was used by the ACCEPTS developers to assess referred children's classroom behavior and peer-to-peer social behavior in free play settings (usually the playground during recess periods). While the ACCEPTS Checklist provides information on qualitative aspects of the child's behavior in classroom and playground settings, the observational measure directly records the amount of time the child follows classroom rules and participates socially with peers. Whenever possible, it is advised that the ACCEPTS Observation Form (see Appendix 7) be used to record both classroom behavior and social behavior on the playground during either free play or structured activities. Information from the checklist combined with direct observation provides a comprehensive picture of the child's classroom and social adjustments. Instructions for using these instruments in the screening process are described under *Screening Procedures* below.

Screening Procedures

A first step in the screening process involves disseminating information about the ACCEPTS program to all school personnel who are in a position to either refer children or make judgments about their classroom and/or social behavior. The overview of the ACCEPTS program presented earlier can be used for this purpose. The overview material can be distributed to all appropriate school or district level staff and referrals coordinated through a central point such as a school counselor or special education office.

Individual teachers (either regular or special education) or school psychological personnel can also initiate the ACCEPTS social skills training program themselves and conduct the appropriate initial assessments. In such instances, it would not be necessary to disseminate program information to others in order to initiate screening procedures.

As noted, all classroom teachers who have concerns about a child's social-behavioral deficits should complete Sections I and II of the ACCEPTS Checklist to obtain as complete a picture as possible of his/her behavioral status. Selected adult supervisors of playground and free play settings should also complete Section II of the Checklist. Each rater should carefully read the rater instructions contained in the ACCEPTS Checklist (See Appendix 6).

If at all possible, direct observations of the child's classroom behavior and social behavior in free play settings should be recorded by the classroom teacher, an aide, a recess supervisor, a school counselor, or other professional, e.g., school psychologist, social worker, and so forth. Ideally, two to three classroom and two to three recess periods should be sampled on different school days. That is, one classroom and one recess period should be observed in a single day, until two to three each have been sampled. The classroom and recess periods observed in should be 15 to 30 minutes in length.

At this point, turn to Appendix 7 and study carefully the ACCEPTS Observation Form and Accompanying Record Form and note carefully the instructions for recording classroom and peer-to-peer social behavior. A stopwatch is used to record the child's classroom and playground behavior and produces valuable information about adjustment in these two settings. This method is accurate, easy to use, and unobtrusive, and, in the authors' opinions, is well worth the time and effort.

It is recommended that classroom and playground periods be observed where the child's behavior is known to be deficient or a problem. If possible, conduct observations in the same periods each day to gauge consistency and to provide an adequate sample of behavior for determining eligibility.

Sometimes it is helpful to graph the classroom and playground observations so that patterns of performance can be evaluated. Some hypothetical recordings are graphed below.
The classroom sessions and the playground sessions should each be averaged to obtain an overall figure for use in determining selection.

It should be noted that the ACCEPTS Checklist and observation form can be used both during and after the program to assess the performance of children who are selected. If time permits, the reader is encouraged to use the instruments for this purpose.

Selection Criteria

Standards or criteria are presented below for using the ACCEPTS Checklist and observation information in selecting target children. Better decisions will be made if both sources of information are used.

The Checklist provides information about the child's behavioral quality and the Observation Form yields information on behavioral level. For example, some children have appropriate social skills, but interact at very low rates, while others with deficient skills interact at high rates—although inappropriately. Both types of children could benefit greatly from the social skills training provided by the ACCEPTS curriculum.

Children should be selected for the *classroom*

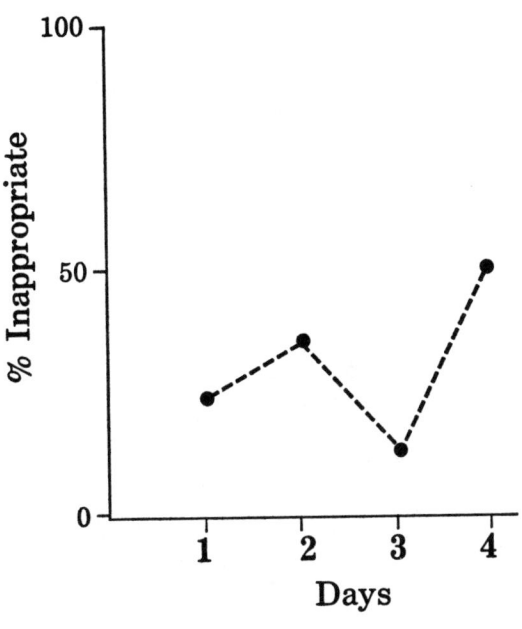
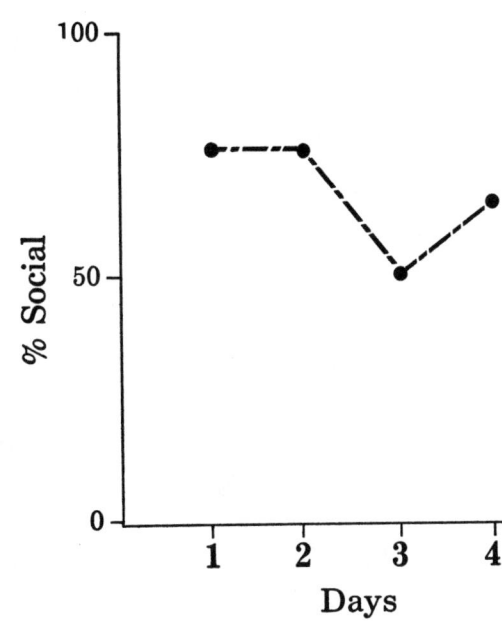

skills training component of the ACCEPTS curriculum if they:

(1) Have *two or more* of the items in Section I of the ACCEPTS Checklist checked "yes", or

(2) Average 25% or more of the time observed, across the observation periods, spent in *inappropriate* behavior (normal children engage in inappropriate classroom behavior 10 to 20% of the time).

Children should be selected for the peer-to-peer social skills training component of the ACCEPTS curriculum if they:

(1) Have *three or more* of the items in Section II of the ACCEPTS Checklist checked as "yes", or

(2) Average 80% of the time or less spent in social participation (normal children socially participate in free play settings 85-90% of the time).

The teacher should complete the ACCEPTS Placement Test in Appendix 8 for children who qualify on either the classroom skills or peer-to-peer social criteria. This test determines which specific skills in the curriculum the child should be taught.

SECTION III
SERVICE DELIVERY OPTIONS AND STAFF TRAINING

The purpose of this section is to describe ACCEPTS service delivery options and staff training procedures. ACCEPTS was designed originally to systematically teach essential social skills to handicapped children and to be as self-instructional as possible. However, the program has a variety of important uses in serving the needs of both handicapped and nonhandicapped children. It is also useful for involved staff to receive as much pre-training and exposure to the program as possible. These two topics are addressed separately below.

Service Delivery Options

There are a number of service delivery options that can be considered in using the ACCEPTS program. The feasibility of different options is influenced by such factors as the nature or severity of the target child's deficits, the settings in which child behavior is problematic, the number of children in need of social skills training, staff availability, the amount of teacher time that can be devoted to the program, and daily instructional time that can be made available for teaching the curriculum. The three major delivery options that can be considered are (1) to teach the curriculum content only, (2) to apply the behavior management procedures only, and (3) to teach the curriculum and apply behavior management procedures. Each is described below.

Teaching the Curriculum Only

There will be numerous occasions where it is feasible to teach the ACCEPTS curriculum content without implementing behavior management procedures. This is particularly true when the program is used with nonhandicapped children.

There are four different arrangements or types of instruction for teaching the curriculum. These are 1 to 1, small group, large group, or the entire classroom. 1 to 1 instruction is more demanding of the teacher, but provides for the most intensive teaching of curriculum content. It can be considered for use with very deficient children who have difficulty in discriminating when to use key skills and when they are applying them correctly.

Small group instruction is recommended as a highly desirable instructional option. As already noted, research suggests that this is a most effective format for teaching social skills (La Greca & Santogrossi, 1980). Small group teaching can be used with several (two to four/five) handicapped children of approximately equal deficit levels. When there is only one handicapped child, small group teaching can be used most effectively by involving several nonhandicapped children as peer tutors who may be in need of social skills training.

Large group instruction is appropriate for use in special education settings such as resource and self-contained classrooms. In applications of this type it may be helpful to form several large groups of children whose social skills deficits are similar or at the same general level and to instruct them separately. Careful formation of such groups can make the instructional process much easier to manage. However, the number of groups should be held to a minimum because of the added burdens imposed by each.

Entire classroom teaching of the curriculum should be considered by regular teachers. The content can be of significant value to the broad range of nonhandicapped children and could be taught as a social studies unit. If the curriculum has been taught to a handicapped child who is or will be mainstreamed, it is highly recommended that his/her nonhandicapped peers be exposed to it also. This could greatly facilitate the mainstreaming and effective integration of handicapped children and also contribute to a better overall classroom atmosphere.

Activities and teaching examples for each of these four instructional arrangements are built into the curriculum (see Section V). The teaching guidelines and instructions described in Section IV should be followed carefully in using each arrangement.

Applying the Behavior Management Procedures Only

There are children who are socially skilled and can display classroom behavioral competencies appropriately. However, for sometimes obscure reasons, they choose not to apply their skills. Such children are in need of behavior management procedures to provide feedback, incentives, and practice in producing them. The ACCEPTS behavior management procedures are perfectly suited for use in these situations.

The ACCEPTS behavior management procedures can be used to achieve general behavior change/remediation goals in the school setting. For example, the classroom procedures can be used to increase the level of appropriate classroom behavior of children in general. Similarly, the playground procedures can be used in a variety of ways, e.g., to increase the social contact and participation of socially withdrawn children or to improve the quality (e.g., positive or negative) of children's social interactions with peers.

Teaching the Curriculum and Applying Behavior Management Procedures Simultaneously

The greatest overall impact on child behavior is accomplished with this delivery option. However, it is also the most time consuming.

Behavior management procedures should be applied in conjunction with the curriculum when it is apparent that the target child needs practice and training in applying previously taught skills in natural settings. It is possible that some children would need practice/training in peer-to-peer skills and not classroom behavioral competencies or vice versa. These judgments will have to be made on a case-by-case basis.

As a rule, behavior management procedures should be applied in the classroom near the end of instruction in the first section of the curriculum, e.g., Classroom Skills. The playground behavior management procedures should be introduced as soon as instruction begins in the peer-to-peer skills. Both management systems should remain in effect until all instruction in the curriculum is completed (see Section VI for details on fading out the ACCEPTS behavior management systems).

Relationships between these three service delivery options and demands on the teacher and program outcomes are summarized in the table below.

Table 1 suggests that the more comprehensive the ACCEPTS program implementation, the greater will be the benefits to the target child. This assumption is, of course, based on a consistently high quality implementation effort. Staff training procedures, to be described below, are directly related to this issue.

Staff Training Procedures

Whenever possible, users of the ACCEPTS program should receive pre-training in its implementation. The program authors conducted a number of staff training workshops in field testing the program. These inservice training sessions lasted either one or two full days and were attended by regular and special education teachers, psychologists,

TABLE 1

ACCEPTS Service Delivery Options, Teacher Demands, and Program Outcomes

Service Delivery Option	Demands on Classroom Teacher	Impact on Conceptual Mastery of Social Skills	Impact on Use of Skills in Natural Settings	Impact on Overall Social and Classroom Adjustment
Social Skills Instruction Only	Low	High	Low	Low to Medium
Behavior Management Procedures Only	Low to Medium	Low	High	Medium to High
Social Skills Instruction and Behavior Management Procedures	Medium to High	High	High	High

school administrators, counselors, social workers, and speech therapists.

The availability of such workshops is limited and would, in most cases, not be available prior to program implementation. This section presents information that will be of value to you in preparing yourself to implement the program, and training others to use it.

Self-Training Procedures

As noted earlier, the ACCEPTS program was designed to be sufficiently self-instructional so that school personnel could apply it without formal training. To date, there have been a number of successful applications of the program under these conditions.

However, to facilitate both staff and self-training procedures, the authors are developing a model implementation videotape of the ACCEPTS program. The videotape will cover the following topics:

(1) A brief overview of the literature on *mainstreaming, social skills training,* and *the relationship of social adjustment, competence,* and *peer acceptance* to long-term development.

(2) A parent-teacher conference in which a teacher consultant explains the ACCEPTS program and the parents', teachers', and consultants' role in it.

(3) A consultant-teacher conference in which the target child's behavior problems and the referring teacher's concerns are dealt with. Tasks the teacher must complete daily are explained and discussed.

(4) The consultant explaining the ACCEPTS program to the target child.

(5) The consultant explaining the recess incentive program to the target child's peers with the target child present.

(6) The consultant conducting social skills training with the target child using a 1-to-1 instructional format.

(7) The referring teacher applying the classroom behavior management procedures.

(8) The consultant on the playground coaching, providing feedback, praising, and awarding free-time minutes for the child's performance.

(9) The target child and a selected peer consuming earned freetime working on a puzzle.

The tape will be approximately one-hour in length and divided into the above segments. Write to the publisher for information on the availability of the tape. If possible, you are urged to preview this tape before implementing the program and to refer to it on an as-needed basis during implementation.

Also, before attempting to implement the program, it is essential that you become thoroughly familiar with all the remaining material in this volume, e.g., Sections IV-VI plus Appendices. As a final preparation, it is recommended that you practice several of the instructional formats before beginning instruction.

Staff Training Procedures

In developing and validating a series of behavior management packages over an eight-year period, the senior author and his colleagues (Walker, Hops & Greenwood, in press) developed and tested a workshop training format that focused on both *conceptual* and *behavioral* mastery of the programs. This format is recommended for your consideration in training other staff to use the ACCEPTS program in a workshop situation and is described below. Before attempting to train others, you should apply the ACCEPTS program at least once. The following topics should be covered in the workshop:

(1) The importance of social skills training and its relationship to child development and adjustment capability (e.g., the material in Section I).

(2) Procedures for screening and identifying appropriate candidates for the program.

(3) Instructional Guidelines and Procedures.

(4) The teaching scripts and curriculum content.

(5) Behavior management procedures.

Each of these components should be taught using the following teaching procedure.

Step One
Assign the appropriate material in this volume to read and provide a brief overview of the main points relating to the component being taught.

Step Two
Answer questions and discuss the material read.

Step Three
Show the segment of the ACCEPTS model implementation tape dealing with the component or task.

Step Four
Provide opportunities for role playing and/or practicing applying the component.

Step Five
Answer questions and discuss applications as appropriate.

Repeat this teaching procedure for each of the major workshop topics referred to above. Training can be delivered in either a one or two day format, depending upon group size and other factors.

SECTION IV
GUIDELINES FOR TEACHING THE ACCEPTS CURRICULUM

This section contains instructions and guidelines for teaching the ACCEPTS curriculum. The topics covered include:

(1) *The Placement Test:* Procedures for determining which skills to teach.
(2) *The Reference List:* How to identify each skill and its corresponding teaching script.
(3) *The Instructional Sequence:* An overview of the basic teaching steps contained in each script.
(4) *The Teaching Scripts:* Instructions for using the teaching scripts.
(5) *The Review Scripts:* Instructions for using the review scripts.
(6) *The Correction Procedure:* How to correct mistakes during instruction.
(7) *Behavior Management:* Suggestions for managing students during instructional sessions.
(8) *Review:* Teacher checklist of major steps to follow in beginning ACCEPTS instruction.

The ACCEPTS Placement Test

A placement test for the ACCEPTS curriculum is contained in Appendix 8 for use in identifying which of the 28 skills to teach. There will be some children whose social skills repertoire is so deficient that they should be exposed to the entire curriculum from start to finish. Any child whose placement profile indicates they are deficient in 75% or more (21+) of the skills should receive instruction in the entire curriculum.

The target handicapped child's social skills repertoire should be rated on the placement test by the teacher most familiar with his/her behavior pattern. If a handicapped child is in a self-contained classroom, but will be trained by the school counselor, the special education teacher should do the rating. Ideally, the person doing the rating and the training should be the same.

A Likert scale was applied to the 28 social skills to form the placement test (see example below). There is a one-to-one correspondence between the items assessed on the placement test and the social skills contained in the ACCEPTS curriculum.

The rater assesses the child's skill or behavioral level on a five-point scale for each item in the test. The rating reflects the degree to which the item's content is descriptive of the target child's behavior. For example, an item on the placement test might read as follows:

THE STUDENT SHARES LAUGHTER WITH CLASSMATES

Not Descriptive or True	Moderately Descriptive or True	Very Descriptive or True
1 . . . . . . 2 . . . . . . 3 . . . . . . 4 5		

A rating of four or above on this scale indicates a satisfactory level of competence on performance on the skill. A rating of one or two indicates very deficient performance. A rating of *three* or less strongly suggests the child should receive instruction in that behavior or skill.

If the rater is not comfortable in judging the target child's performance on a particular skill because of insufficient observation or information, it would be possible to present one of the criterion role play situations for that skill (see teaching scripts) and assess performance under these stimulus conditions. The child's performance in the role play situation would simulate actual conditions in which the skill's use would be called for. It would also be possible to expose a nonhandicapped peer to the same role play situation to provide a comparative standard for judging the target child's performance.

Appendix 9 contains a Summary Sheet for collating the child's rating on the placement test and determining which skills should be targeted for instruction. Each item on the placement test is referred to on the Summary Sheet by *AREA* and by *NUMBER* with spaces provided to record the item ratings. Also included on the Summary Sheet is a listing of the specific ACCEPTS social skills corresponding to the placement test items. As mentioned, any item given a rating of *three or less* should be taught.

The ACCEPTS Reference List

The reference list (see Appendix 2) is composed of the 28 ACCEPTS skills grouped into five instructional areas. Each skill is identified by skill *AREA*, skill *NUMBER*, and skill *NAME*. The reference list serves as a table of contents for the teaching scripts. For each skill there is a corresponding *TEACHING SCRIPT PAGE NUMBER*

EXAMPLE:

(Skill Area)
↓
Area II: Basic Interaction Skills
(Skill Number) → 1. Eye Contact........Page_____
↑ ↑
(Skill Name) (Teaching Script Page Number)

In addition, the reference list provides page numbers for five *AREA REVIEWS*. These refer the teacher to the review scripts to be used after all skills in an instructional area have been taught.

The ACCEPTS Instructional Sequence

The ACCEPTS instructional sequence was modeled after a direct instruction teaching procedure. By following scripted formats, each of the 28 ACCEPTS skills is taught individually with a maximum of nine instructional steps. The basic instructional sequence is standardized across all 28 teaching scripts, however, the actual number of steps involved in the instructional sequence varies according to individual skill difficulty. The basic instructional sequence outlined below includes the maximum number of teaching steps contained in any one teaching script.

Step 1: Definition and Guided Discussion
a. Teacher presents skill definition followed by student oral responding.
b. Teacher leads students in a guided discussion of skill application and a range of examples.

Step 2: Positive Example
a. Teacher presents first video scene example showing appropriate skill application,
or
b. Teacher models an example of appropriate skill application.
c. Debrief episode.

Step 3: Negative Example
a. Teacher presents second video scene (nonexample) demonstrating failure to use skill or incorrect skill application,
or
b. Teacher models a nonexample demonstrating failure to use skill or incorrect skill application.
c. Debrief episode.

Step 4: Review and Restate Skill Definition
a. Teacher reviews skill definition.
b. Student oral responding.

Step 5: Positive Example
a. Teacher presents a third video scene example of appropriate skill application,
or
b. Teacher models a second example of appropriate skill application.
c. Debrief episode.

Step 6: Activities
a. Teacher *models* a range of activities that exemplify and/or expand upon skill production.
b. Teacher presents students with *practice* activities and roleplay situations designed to build skill mastery.

Step 7: Positive Example
a. Teacher presents final video example if called for in the script,
or
b. Teacher models final positive example as needed.
c. Debrief as needed.

Step 8: Criterion Role Plays
a. Teacher presents students with criterion role play calling for skill demonstration.
b. Teacher judges student's quality of skill performance. If acceptable, proceed to next step. If unacceptable, recycle student(s) through an abbreviated instructional sequence, present a second roleplay, and reassess students' performance.

Step 9: Informal Contracting
a. Teacher presents students with a situation or rule for trying out the skill in a natural situation prior to the next session.
b. Students respond with a verbal commitment.

The ACCEPTS Teaching Scripts

The teaching scripts are identified by skill *AREA*, skill *NUMBER*, and skill *NAME*, just as they are in the reference list.

The scripts are organized so that the classroom skills are taught first, followed by the peer-to-peer social skills. For children who are being exposed to the full curriculum, it is important to teach the skills in the order they appear in the reference list. This is necessary because certain skills will require mastery of "preskills" before they can be taught. Preskills are those ACCEPTS skills which have been previously taught or which the student already performed when placed in the program. Where preskills are necessary before teaching a new skill, the teaching scripts will identify them by number.

Each of the 28 teaching scripts contains a sequential order of teaching steps. As noted previously, the basic instructional sequence is standardized across all 28 scripts, however, the number of steps required to teach each skill varies somewhat. In order to use the teaching scripts, the teacher must follow each step in the sequence as well as understand the following notation:
(1) That which appears in "quotes" indicates what the teacher is to say to the students.
(2) That which appears in CAPITAL LETTERS indicates how the students are to respond.
(3) That which appears in (parentheses) indicates instructions to the teacher.

Nearly all the ACCEPTS skills have accompanying video scenes that are used in conjunction with the teaching scripts. Skill names on the video tape are identical to those in the reference list and follow the same sequence.

The Teaching Scripts which do have accompanying video scenes identify where and when these scenes are to be presented during instruction. However, if video equipment is unavailable, alternative teaching examples are provided (see Appendix 10) and can be substituted for the steps outlined in the teaching scripts which ordinarily would call for video scenes.

A sample of one of the ACCEPTS Teaching Scripts designed to teach the skill *Starting* is presented below along with instructions for using the scripts. This example should be studied carefully before beginning the formal teaching process and should serve as a model for your teaching behavior vis-a-vis the ACCEPTS curriculum. Since the example script is accompanied by instructions, refer to the actual Teaching Script used for *Starting* as a final self-check and review of scripted notation.

TEACHING SCRIPT EXAMPLE: Instructions for Using the Teaching Scripts

AREA I e.g., Basic Interaction Skills

SKILL #3 e.g., Starting

PRESKILLS: AREA II, 1-2

REVIEW: This section is included for the purpose of reviewing previously taught skills: e.g., Brief discussion of previous day's skill. Check to see if the students followed the informal contract.

Step 1: DEFINITION AND GUIDED DISCUSSION

Definition:

1. Teacher provides skill definition: e.g., "Starting means finding someone to talk to."
2. Teacher asks students' definition. Use of hand signals to indicate when students are to respond is appropriate: e.g., "What does starting mean?"
3. Students respond in unison: e.g., FINDING SOMEONE TO TALK TO
4. Teacher reinforces correct response or corrects an incorrect response. See Appendix 11 for samples of *reinforcing statements*. e.g., (reinforce or correct)
5. Teacher presents skill definition another way: e.g., "Let's say this another way. Finding someone to talk to is called *starting*."
6. Teacher asks students' definition another way: e.g., "Finding someone to talk to is called what?"
7. Students respond in unison: e.g., STARTING
8. Teacher *reinforces* correct response or goes through *correction procedure*. e.g., (reinforce or correct).
9. Teacher presents subsequent scripted examples followed by student oral responding. Teacher provides *reinforcement* or goes through *correction procedure* as needed: e.g., "Let's try some more. Sam was on the playground. Sam found someone to talk to. Sam was doing what?"
STARTING (reinforce or correct)
"How do we know Sam was starting?"
HE/SAM FOUND SOMEONE TO TALK TO (reinforce or correct)
"You are having free time. You find someone to talk to. You are doing what?"
STARTING (reinforce or correct)

Guided Discussion:

1. Teacher provides more information about the skill: e.g., "Starting is the first thing you need to do to make a friend. This is how you start: First, you find a person to talk to."
2. Teacher tests students' comprehension of information by asking for a translation, or in some cases, application questions: e.g., "When you start, what do you do first?"
3. Students respond in unison: e.g., FIND A PERSON TO TALK TO
4. Teacher *reinforces* correct response or goes through *correction procedure*: e.g., (reinforce or correct)
5. Student/Teacher discussion continues. Examples of ways to use the skill may be asked for or given by the teacher. Provide *reinforcement* or go through *correction procedure* as needed: e.g., "Next, you should look at the person and say something. What should you do next?"
LOOK AT THE PERSON AND SAY SOMETHING (reinforce or correct)
"Saying hello to a new student in your class is one way of starting. Asking a person what their name is is another way of starting. What are some other ways to start?" (Discuss, suggest examples such as asking the person to play, etc.). "How do you get to talk and play with people?"
STARTING (reinforce or correct)
Note:
The guided discussions on all the teaching scripts are intended to be informal exchanges between student(s) and teacher. Teachers may wish to encourage student(s) to think of applications of the skill in their own activities. Often, in the interest of promoting discussion, the teacher may not wish to follow the formal correction procedure when errors are made. Instead, the teacher may choose to: (a) accept an approximation of a correct response, (b)

provide the student with a correct response, or (c) call on another student.

Step 2: POSITIVE EXAMPLE

1. Nearly all the teaching scripts have an accompanying video scene which will be used to model a positive example of the skill, i.e., a demonstration of appropriate skill application: e.g., Video: Positive example

Note:
A. There are a few teaching scripts that will not have an accompanying video scene/example. Where a video scene is not called for in the script, the teacher is provided with instructions for modeling an example of the skill. These instructions are provided directly on the script itself.
B. If you have *not* purchased the video tapes that accompany the ACCEPTS curriculum or do not have video equipment available, you should *not* skip the steps which call for presentation of examples. Rather, where video examples are called for on the script, you can substitute live modeling demonstrations by the teacher or a *skilled* group of students. Each video scene which has been prepared for this purpose is described briefly in Appendix 10. These descriptions provide a basis for determining appropriate examples to be modeled.

2. Following presentation of the positive video or live model example, the teacher leads students in brief discussion of what occurred. e.g., (Debrief: Point out/discuss why example was a positive instance of the skill).

Step 3: NEGATIVE EXAMPLE

1. Again, nearly all the teaching scripts have an accompanying video scene which will be used to model a negative example (nonexample) of the skill, i.e., incorrect skill application or failure to use the skill: e.g., Video: Negative example

Note:
A. The same instructions apply here regarding live modeling of the example as were described in Step 2. (See Step 2, Notes A and B).

B. A few of the skills are taught "to the positive side only." That is, negative examples have not been included in the instructional sequence.

2. Following presentation of the negative video or live model example, the teacher leads students in a brief discussion of what occurred: e.g., (Debrief: Point out/discuss why example was *not* a positive instance of the skill).

Step 4: REVIEW AND RESTATE DEFINITION

1. Teacher repeats a definition of the skill: e.g., "Finding someone to talk to is *starting*."
2. Teacher asks students the definition: e.g., "Finding someone to talk to is what?"
3. Students respond in unison: e.g., STARTING
4. Teacher *reinforces* correct response or goes through *correction procedure*: e.g., (reinforce or correct)

Step 5: POSITIVE EXAMPLE

1. Refer to instructions provided in Step 2. Video: Positive example (Debrief: Point out/discuss why example is a positive instance of the skill).

Step 6: ACTIVITIES

Teacher Models:

1. Teacher models the skill as indicated on the script: e.g., (Select a student to 'start' with. Place the student at a distance). "Watch me and see how I can do starting. Let's say I'm on the playground playing by myself. I see you over there. Pretend I don't know you, but I want to play with you." (Teacher looks around the room, sees student, and walks over). "Hi, my name is _____, what's your name? Trading names is one way to start."
2. Teacher models the skill another way if indicated on the script: (Select another student to "start" with). "Here's another way to start. Let's say our class is going to lunch and we can choose anyone we want to sit by. 'Hi (*student's name*), would you sit by me at lunch?' That time I started by asking (*student's name*) to sit by me."

Students Practice:

1. Teacher provides activities to practice the skill: e.g. (Place students around the room). "O.K. Now you are going to practice starting. Let's say you are all playing by yourself in the classroom. Pretend you don't know each other. When I say 'start', go find a person to talk to." (Give students the cue to 'start'. Make sure everyone gets a chance to initiate. Prompt different ways of starting, if needed).
2. *Reinforce* appropriate responses or go through *correction procedure:* e.g., (reinforce or correct as needed).
3. Teacher provides students with remaining practice activities. *Reinforce* or go through *correction procedure* as needed: e.g., (Arrange chairs in a row by twos. Pair off students. Seat half the partners in the chairs, leaving an adjacent empty chair for the partner. Have the other partners form a line). "O.K. Let's pretend you are getting on the school bus to ride home. It's the first day of school, so let's say you don't know anyone on the bus yet. I want this group to get on the bus and sit by your partner. Remember, you don't know your partner. Show me how you would use starting." (Reinforce "starting" or correct. Switch places and have the other group get on the bus).
4. Etc.
5. Etc.

Step 7: POSITIVE EXAMPLE

1. Refer to instructions provided in *Step 2:* Video: Positive example (Debrief: Point out/discuss why example is a positive instance of the skill).

Note:
   This final positive example is only called for on a few of the teaching scripts.

Step 8: CRITERION ROLE PLAYS

1. Teacher presents student(s) with *any one* of the three criterion role plays to test skill mastery: e.g., (Pair off students): "Let's pretend both you and your partner are new students in the class. The teacher has just told everyone that it's free time. Show me how you would 'start' so you can get to know each other."
2. Teacher judges skill mastery. Student demonstration of the skill called for in the role play is judged by means of a "criterion" or standard for acceptable performance: e.g., (*Criterion:* Students initiate 'starting' with each other which includes trading names).
3. The purpose of the criterion role play is to assess skill mastery. In the event of an incorrect response, i.e., unacceptable skill performance, the correction procedure referred to on all other sections of the teaching scripts is not used. Rather, the student is recycled through an abbreviated instructional sequence until mastery performance is achieved.

   Presentation of the role plays and use of the abbreviated instructional sequence is determined as follows:

a. Select *one* of the three role plays provided to present first. If student performance meets the criterion indicated, proceed to the final step indicated on the script (Informal Contracting).
b. If student performance on the first role play *does not* meet the criterion indicated, reteach the *Definitional* sequence as presented in Step 1. Then present a second role play. If performance on the second role play meets the criterion indicated, proceed to the final step indicated on the script (Informal Contracting).
c. If student performance on a second role play *does not* meet the criterion indicated, reteach the skill using the following abbreviated sequence:
   (1) Reteach the *Definitional* sequence as presented in Step 1, *and*
   (2) Reteach the *Activities* sequence as presented on this script in Step 6.
After reteaching, present a third role play. If student performance meets the criterion indicated, proceed to the final step indicated on the script (*Informal Contracting*).
d. If student performance on a third role play *does not* meet the criterion indicated, recylce the student through the abbreviated *Instructional* sequence again (see above, 3c). Then re-present any role play. Continue until mastery performance is achieved (*Note:* If the student's level of functioning is too low, the instructional procedure may be inappropriate).
e. *Exception:* A number of the more complex AC-

CEPTS skills require more than one "criterion" for determining acceptable performance. In such cases, more than one role play must be presented in order to assess mastery of all components of the skill. The Criterion Role Plays for these skills are identified on the scripts as "Criterion Role Play Sets". The students' performance of the skill must then meet each criterion indicated within the Role Play Set. When performance does not meet each criterion indicated within the Role Play Set, recycle the student through the abbreviate instructional procedures as described above (see 3a-d).

The ACCEPTS Review Scripts

Systematic review of the ACCEPTS skills which have been previously taught via the Teaching Scripts will be important for ensuring skill mastery and maintaining levels of skilled behavior.

There are five Area Review Scripts which accompany the 28 Teaching Scripts. The Review Scripts are identified by area NUMBER and area NAME:

Area I Review:	Classroom Skills
Area II Review:	Basic Interaction Skills
Area III Review:	Getting Along Skills
Area IV Review:	Making Friends Skills
Area V Review:	Coping Skills

The Review Scripts are intended for use *after* all skills in a particular instructional area have been taught and are located accordingly in the text.

In each Area Review lesson, the students and teacher briefly review the skill definitions and practice each of the skills in that area. The teacher then presents a slightly more complex role play situation than those used for the criterion role plays. The student must decide which skill or skills to role play at each step in the situation.

The scripted notations (i.e., quotation marks, capitals, and parenthesis) used in the Teaching Scripts also apply to the Review Scripts.

A sample of one of the Area Review Scripts used for *Making Friends* is presented below along with instructions for its use. This example should be studied carefully before beginning an actual review lesson. Since the example Area Review Script is accompanied by instructions, refer to the actual Review Script used for *Making Friends Skills* as a final self-check and review of scripted notation.

REVIEW SCRIPT EXAMPLE
Instructions for Using Review Scripts

AREA IV REVIEW: MAKING FRIENDS SKILLS

Step 1: RULE REVIEW AND PRACTICE

Rule Review:

1.1. Teacher presents first skill definition: e.g., "Good grooming means being neat and clean".
2. Teacher asks students the definition: e.g., "Being neat and clean is called what?"
3. Students respond in unison: e.g., GOOD GROOMING
4. Teacher reinforces a correct response *or* goes through correction procedure for an incorrect response: e.g., (Reinforce or correct)
5. Teacher asks students to further define skill.

Practice:

e.g., "What are some things you should do to be neat and clean?"
6. Students respond with examples: e.g., WASH HANDS AND FACE, BRUSH TEETH, WEAR CLEAN CLOTHES, etc.
7. Teacher reinforces correct responses *or* goes through correction procedure for incorrect response: e.g., (Reinforce or correct)

Rule Review:

2.1. Teacher presents second skill definition: e.g., "Smiling shows you like someone or are having fun."

2. Teacher asks students the definition: e.g., "How do you show you like someone or are having fun?"
3. Students respond in unison: e.g., SMILE
4. Teacher reinforces a correct response *or* goes through correction procedure for an incorrect response: e.g. (Reinforce or correct)

Practice:

5. Teacher provides an activity in which the students are to demonstrate use of the skill: e.g., "Let's *do it*. Pretend we are all playing together and having a good time!"
6. Students demonstrate skill: e.g., (Students smile)
7. Teacher reinforces correct response *or* goes through correction procedure for an incorrect response: e.g., (Reinforce or correct)

Rule review and practice is continued for remaining skills:

Rule Review:

3.1. "Saying what you like about a person is complimenting."
2. "Saying what you like about a person is called what?"
3. COMPLIMENTING
4. (Reinforce or correct).

Practice:

5. (Pair off students). "O.K. I want everybody to give your partner a compliment."
6. (Students give a compliment to each other. Reinforce or correct).

Rule Review:

4.1. "Making friends means starting, taking turns talking, and inviting."
2. "What do you do when you make friends?"
3. START, TAKE TURNS TALKING, AND INVITE.
4. (Reinforce or correct)

Practice:

5. (Pair off students). "Pretend you don't know your partner and show me how you would make friends. First, start by trading names. Then, take turns talking about things you both like to do. Then, invite the person to spend time with you."
6. (Students demonstrate friendship making sequence. Reinforce or correct).

Step 2: ROLE PLAY

1. Teacher discusses application of skill with students: "Here's a chance to use all the Making Friends skills. First, let's talk about good grooming."
2. Teacher gives students feedback about skill application: e.g., (If student is neat and clean, give specific praise. If grooming could be improved, give specific suggestions).
3. Teacher presents role play situation to test students' ability to apply skills to daily activities: e.g., (Pair off students). "Next, let's pretend you and your partner are sitting next to each other on a bus going on a field trip. Let's say you don't know each other, but you want to make friends. While you are taking turns talking I'd also like you to show that you are having a good time together and to give each other a compliment."
4. Students demonstrate skills: e.g., (Students trade names, take turns talking, invite, smile, and compliment).
5. Teacher reinforces correct responses *or* reteaches skills as needed: e.g., (Reinforce making friends, smiling, complimenting, *or* reteach skills as needed).

The ACCEPTS Correction Procedure

An essential component to effective teaching with the ACCEPTS Curriculum is to provide students with continuous feedback on their performance during instruction. The scripted teaching formats were designed to include the notation "(Reinforce or correct)" as a cue for the teacher to provide immediate feedback following any given response/nonresponse. Feedback from the teacher should include either: a) reinforcement/praise following a correct response, or b) correction following response errors.

The ACCEPTS correction procedure was developed for the purpose of correcting response errors. Two major types of response errors can occur during instruction. These are: (1) the student(s) can give an *incorrect response*, or (2) the student(s) can give *no response*. Either error can occur in: (a) the student's conceptual understanding of the skill and its definition (verbal type) and (b) the students' ability to demonstrate the skill in a roleplay/practice situation (demonstration type).

The ACCEPTS correction procedure is implemented immediately after a student(s') response error and follows a basic *model, lead, test* format. The procedure is briefly summarized as follows:

A. Student(s): Response Errors:
1. Incorrect response
or
2. No response

B. Teacher: Correction Procedure:
1. *Model* correct response
and
2. *Lead* student(s) through correct response
and
3. *Test* student(s) for correct response.

Whether the teacher is conducting instruction with a small group or individually (i.e., one-to-one), it is very important that response errors be corrected promptly and consistently whenever they occur. The ACCEPTS correction procedure is described below and illustrated on accompanying flowcharts.

Correction Procedure Instructions

The teacher begins the correction procedure immediately following an incorrect student response or no student response to:

1. *Any* scripted question, e.g., "What does *starting* mean?"

or

2. *Any* scripted activity/situation in which the student is to demonstrate/practice the skill, e.g., "... pretend you don't know your partner. Show me how you would *start*."

The correction procedure for: (1) an incorrect verbal response *or* an incorrect demonstration response, and (2) no verbal response or no demonstration response is exemplified as follows:

Step 1: MODEL

A. In the case of an *incorrect response* (either verbal type or demonstration type) first provide the student(s) with information that the response was incorrect (i.e., say "no") then *model* the correct response: *Verbal Example* — "No, *starting* means finding someone to talk to." *Demonstration Example* — "No, watch me and see how I *start*."

B. In the case of *no response* either verbal type or demonstration type) omit "no" and proceed directly to the *model*: *Verbal Example* — "Starting means finding someone to talk to." *Demonstration Example* — "Watch me and see how I *start*."

Step 2: LEAD

Lead the student(s) through the correct response: *Verbal Example* — "Say it with me: *Starting* means finding someone to talk to." *Demonstration Example* — "*Start* with me," or "Do it with me."

Note: Leading a demonstration response should be done in a manner that is appropriate for the situation, i.e., have the student demonstrate with teacher assistance, or do it together, etc.

Step 3: TEST

Test the student(s) for the correct response: *Verbal Example* — "What does *starting* mean? *Demonstration Example* — "Now show me how you would *start* with your partner."

Step 4: REINFORCE or RECYCLE

Given a correct response the teacher provides a reinforcing statement and correction is completed.

Given an incorrect response or no response, the student is recycled through the correction procedure again.

ACCEPTS Correction Procedure

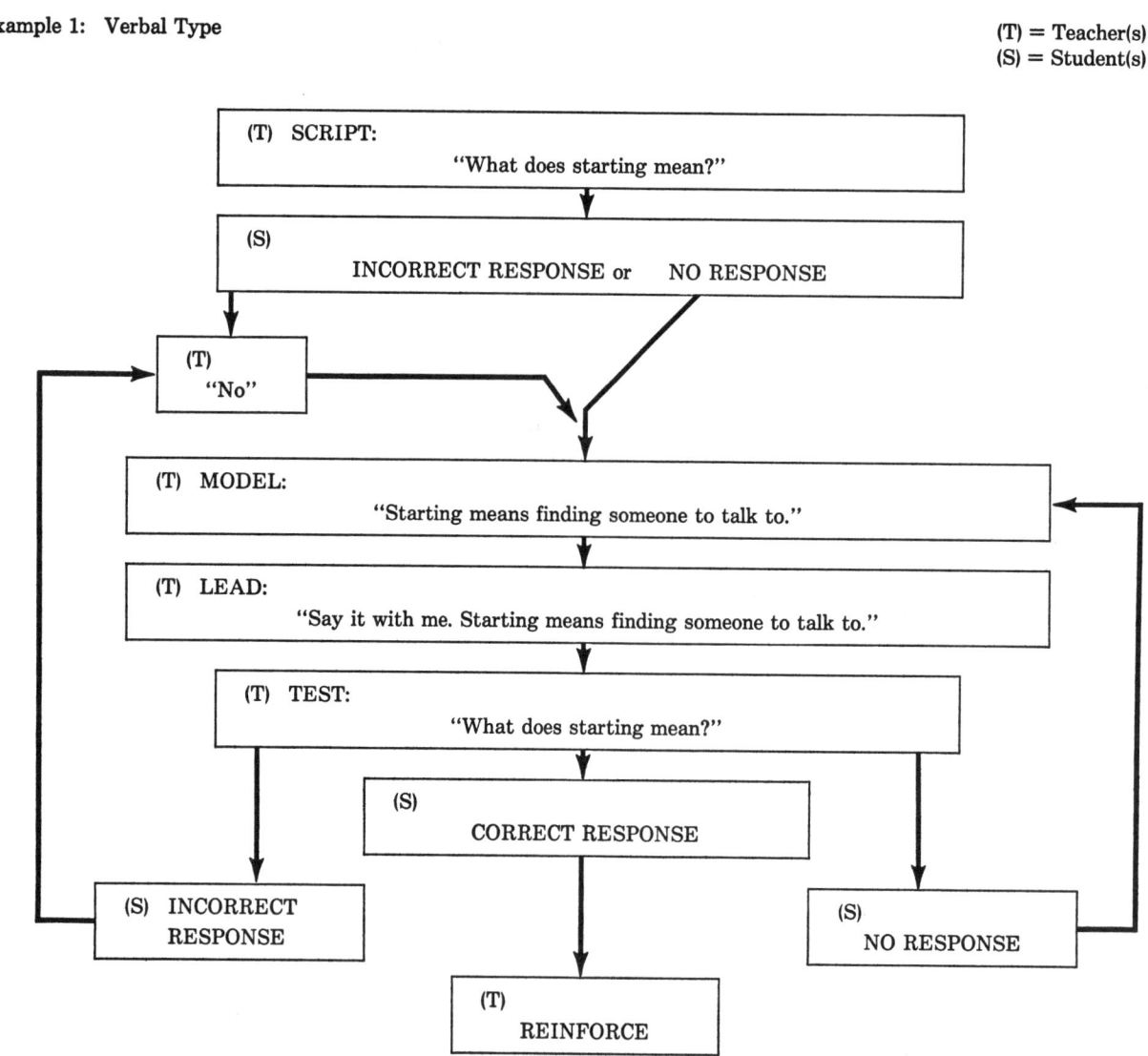

Example 1: Verbal Type

(T) = Teacher(s)
(S) = Student(s)

ACCEPTS Correction Procedure

Example 2: Demonstration Type

(T) = Teacher(s)
(S) = Student(s)

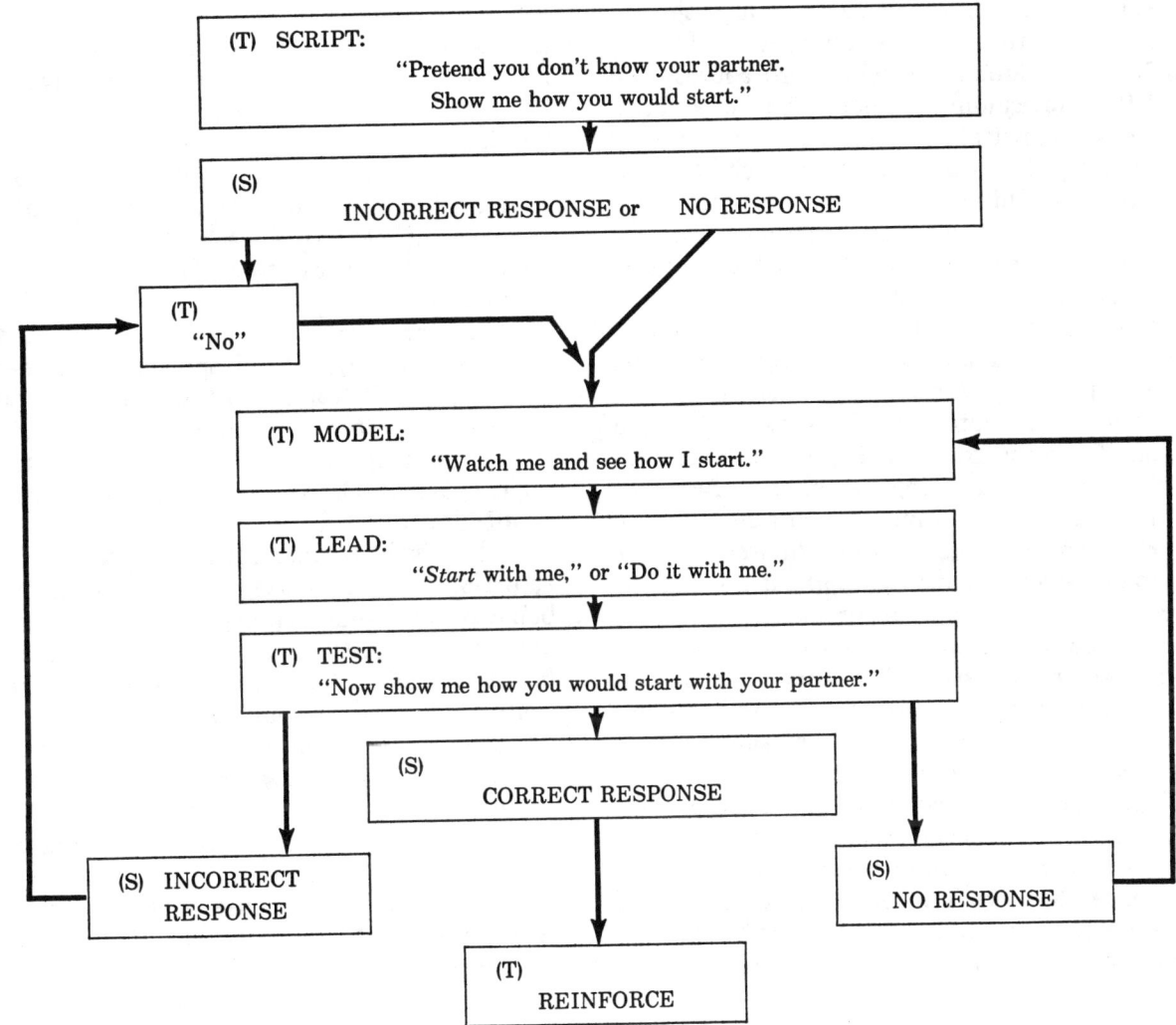

ACCEPTS Behavior Management

Systematic behavior management procedures play an important role in the ACCEPTS program and serve the following purposes: (1) to motivate children to respond to the program, (2) to manage child behavior effectively during instructional sessions, and (3) to strengthen the use and application of previously taught social skills within natural settings such as the classroom and playground. The ACCEPTS Behavior Management Procedures Section (VI) details systematic techniques and procedures for achieving goal number three above, e.g., facilitating the use of ACCEPTS social skills in natural settings. This is an extremely important part of the overall ACCEPTS intervention procedure. Further, recently conducted research by Walker et al. (in press) suggests that the combination of social skills training and behavior management procedures is more powerful than social skills training alone..

Goals number one and two are dealt with here because they are especially germane to the ACCEPTS curriculum and teaching procedures. The ACCEPTS curriculum and instructional procedures seem to be intrinsically motivating to the majority of handicapped and nonhandicapped children exposed to them. This is particularly true of the video vignettes, the role playing situations, and the mastery activities built into the teaching scripts.

Throughout the teaching scripts, there are repeated instances in which the student's understanding of, and ability to demonstrate the skills is tested. Teacher praise and approval given for correct performance, approximations of same, or even for honest effort is extremely important in motivating children and facilitating maximum performance (feedback on errors is equally important, with appropriate correction applied immediately). Praise should be used frequently throughout the instructional process. A rate of one praise statement per minute is not unreasonable in a one-to-one or small group teaching situation. Appendix 11 contains a listing of 80 sample praise statements. This list should help you to vary the content and maintain the quality of your praise.

Finally, it helps to point out why it's important for children to learn social skills, e.g., "you get along better with others," "you have more friends," and "school can be more fun." An initial discussion of this topic followed by brief reminders throughout the instructional process can be very helpful in building motivation.

There are some things that can be done to make the instructional process smoother and that may prevent the occurrence of inappropriate behavior. For example, if the small group consists of the target handicapped child and nonhandicapped peers, peers should be selected who are cooperative, interested in being of assistance, and responsive to small group instruction. If the small group consists of all handicapped children, they should be as homogeneous as possible with respect to severity level and ability to respond to instruction.

The following additional measures are recommended for managing the instructional process:

(1) Develop a set of behavioral rules appropriate for small group instruction, e.g., "feet on the floor," "eyes on the teacher," "hands to yourself," "listen carefully," etc. and communicate them to the children.
(2) Use fast-paced, varied presentations.
(3) Monitor the lowest performers carefully and ask them the most questions.
(4) Call for frequent oral responses.
(5) Adapt scripts, where appropriate, to accommodate individual student needs and differing levels of responsiveness.
(6) Use feedback and praising techniques continuously.
(7) Use praise (and/or bonus points if you wish) when the target child spontaneously demonstrates skills taught in the curriculum during the session, e.g., eye contact, listening, answering, smiling, etc. In this way the skill rule and its usage is reinforced by pointing out instances of its use.

There will be numerous instances during instruction that call for the systematic application of behavior management procedures, e.g., non-compliance, inappropriate peer interactions, disruptive behavior, and so forth. Some techniques are presented below for responding to these situations.

(1) *Ignoring*—Certain types of inappropriate child behavior (e.g. minor irritants, non-disruptive attention-getting behaviors) can be effectively ignored if they are maintained primarily by adult attention. Consistent ignoring may cause them to eventually cease or drop in frequency.
(2) *Praise of Appropriate Behavior*—A useful management technique often used in combination with ignoring. One ignores episodes of inappropriate behavior and waits for an instance of appropriate behavior to praise. "Catch the child being good" is the rule in this situation (Becker, 1971).
(3) *Soft Reprimands*—Some researchers advocate the use of soft reprimands spoken privately to the child (Miller, 1975). For some children in some situations, this technique may prove effective. However, an over-reliance on warnings and negatively valenced reprimands may lead one into the "criticism trap" (Becker, 1971) with opposite results of those intended. Further, soft

reprimands would be difficult to use within a small group teaching situation.

(4) *Praise of Appropriate Behavior in a Proximal Student*—A highly effective technique is to publicly praise the appropriate behavior of a student sitting near the student who is misbehaving. This technique teaches that appropriate (not inappropriate) behavior will prompt teacher attention and approval.

(5) *Group Contingency Point System*—When using a small group teaching format, a group contingency can be used effectively to develop appropriate behavior during the session. Divide the session into five minute intervals and tell the students that one point can be earned for each five minutes if everyone follows the rules, e.g., a set of rules that define appropriate behavior during the session. Award or withhold a point at the end of each five minute bloc and explain why the point was awarded or withheld (use an egg timer to mark intervals, if possible). If 80% of the available points are earned, make a brief free time activity or game available at the end of the session (see list of games and activities provided below).

(6) *Individual Reward System*—In this approach, the behavior of each child in the group is evaluated separately for the session (for lower functioning children it is advisable to break the session up into five or ten minute segments and rate performance within each segment). If session rules have been followed at an acceptable level, a happy face sticker is earned (you can also use points, stars, stamps, or strips of paper). If *three* or *four* out of five stickers are earned in a week, a special privilege is earned either in the child's primary classroom or at home. This method requires the cooperation of the child's teacher and/or parents.

(7) *Assertive Discipline Techniques*—An effective technique for inappropriate behavior is to use the assertive discipline method of writing a child's name on the blackboard when an instance of inappropriate behavior occurs and placing a checkmark (✓) beside it for each additional instance of inappropriate behavior. One minute of available or to be earned free time is deducted for each (✓) mark. A variation that can be added is if no students' names have to be written on the board, everyone gets a bonus point, an extra sticker, or five extra minutes of freetime at the end of the session.

(8) *Time Out/Cost Contingency*—For children who consistently display disruptive and/or noncompliant forms of behavior, it may be necessary to use brief time out or set up response cost procedures (fines) to control it. If so, appropriate sources should be consulted before doing so since these procedures can backfire unless applied correctly (see Walker, 1979 or Sulzer & Mayer, 1972)[1,2].

It may be necessary to use combinations of the above procedures for some groups of children. In other situations no *special* management procedures will be required. Usually this decision will be made within the first week of instruction.

A list of games and activities that can be earned during instructional sessions and made available at the end of the sessions is provided below:
— Play cards with the teacher
— Take a walk on the playground with the teacher
— Play jacks or marbles
— Draw on the chalkboard
— Play Hangman
— Let the target child turn off the video monitor and put the tape away
— Blow up balloons and pop them
— Play the piano
— Listen to a short record
— Let child listen to his/her voice on a tape recorder
— Build a tower out of blocks and knock it down
— Play Simon Says or Follow the Leader
— Freeplay (unstructured) time for target child and peers

---

[1] Sulzer and Mayer. *Procedures and Behavior Modification for School Personnel.* New York: Holt, Rinehart & Winston, 1972.

[2] Walker, H.M. *The Acting Out Child: Coping With Classroom Disruption.* Boston, Allyn & Bacon, 1979.

Review

To summarize, there are four major steps to follow when beginning the ACCEPTS instructional process. A teacher checklist of major activities is provided below:

Step 1: Administer the ACCEPTS Placement Test

A. Turn to Appendix 8, read the instructions and complete the teacher ratings section of the Placement Test.
B. Turn to Appendix 9, record your ratings on the Placement Test's Summary Sheet.
C. Place a checkmark beside those items given a rating of *three or less*.
D. Refer to the far right hand "Skills" column for all items check marked. Items check marked will be the ACCEPTS skills a student needs to be taught.

Step 2: Consult the Reference List

A. The Reference List serves as a table of contents for the Teaching Scripts and Area Review Scripts. Identify the ACCEPTS skills which correspond to items check marked on the Summary Sheet.
B. Mark the Teaching Script page numbers you will be using to teach identified skills.

Step 3: Review Curricular Materials

A. Review instructions for using the teaching scripts.
B. Select a teaching script from each area and rehearse the format.
C. Review instructions for using the Review Scripts.
D. Select a Review Script and rehearse the format.
E. Review correction procedure instructions.
F. Practice correction procedure format.
G. Preview video tapes.
H. If you do not have access to the video tapes, turn to Appendix 10. Review descriptions of video scenes that can be modeled as a substitute for positive and negative video examples.

Step 4: Prepare for Instruction

A. Develop small instructional groups.
B. Develop a management plan to use during instruction.
C. Set up video equipment.
D. Go over the Teaching Scripts you will be using prior to conducting each instructional session.

SECTION V
THE ACCEPTS TEACHING SCRIPTS

AREA I: Classroom Skills

SKILL #1: Listening to the Teacher

Step 1: DEFINITION AND GUIDED DISCUSSION

Definition:

"Listening to the teacher means to sit quietly and look at the teacher. What does listening to the teacher mean?"
SIT QUIETLY AND LOOK AT THE TEACHER
"Let's say this another way: Sitting quietly and looking at the teacher is called *listening to the teacher*. Sitting quietly and looking at the teacher is called what?"
LISTENING TO THE TEACHER (Reinforce or correct)
"Let's try some more. Joe is sitting quietly and looking at the teacher. Joe is doing what?"
LISTENING TO THE TEACHER (Reinforce or correct)
"How do we know Joe is listening to the teacher?"
HE/JOE IS SITTING QUIETLY AND LOOKING AT THE TEACHER (Reinforce or correct)
"During math you should be sitting quietly and looking at the teacher. During math you should be doing what?"
LISTENING TO THE TEACHER (Reinforce or correct)

Guided Discussion:

"When a teacher is talking to you or to your class, it is important that you be a good listener. Good listeners sit quietly and look at the teacher so they can hear what the teacher is saying. What do good listeners do?"
SIT QUIETLY AND LOOK AT THE TEACHER (Reinforce or correct)
"If you are listening and paying attention to the teacher, then you will know *what* you are supposed to be doing and *how* you are supposed to do it. Why is it important to listen?"
SO YOU KNOW WHAT TO DO AND HOW TO DO IT (Accept and reinforce close approximations, or correct)

Step 2: POSITIVE EXAMPLE

Video: One positive example (Debrief: Point out/discuss why example is a positive instance of the skill)

Step 3: NEGATIVE EXAMPLE

Video: One negative example (Debrief: Point out/discuss why example is *not* a positive instance of the skill)

Step 4: REVIEW AND RESTATE DEFINITION

"Listening to the teacher means to sit quietly and look at the teacher. What does listening to the teacher mean?"

SIT QUIETLY AND LOOK AT THE TEACHER (Reinforce or correct)

Step 5: POSITIVE EXAMPLE

Video: One positive example (Debrief: Point out/discuss why example is a positive instance of the skill)

Step 6: ACTIVITIES

Teacher Models:

"Watch me and see how I am a good listener. I'll pretend you are the teacher and you are talking. I should sit quietly and look at you like this." (Teacher sits quietly and looks at students)

Students Practice:

1. "Now I want you to show me how *you* can be good listeners. Sit quietly and look at me." (Reinforce sitting quietly and looking at the teacher, or correct)
2. "This time I want you to watch me and tell me if I'm being a good listener. You are the teacher." (Teacher slumps in chair, looks away, and taps on desk).
"Am I being a good listener?"
NO (Reinforce or correct)
"How do you know I'm *not* being a good listener?"
YOU'RE NOT SITTING QUIETLY AND LOOKING AT THE TEACHER or: YOU'RE LOOKING AWAY, MAKING NOISE, etc. (Reinforce or correct)
3. (Teacher sits up straight and looks at students)
"Am I being a good listener now?"
YES (Reinforce or correct)

"How do you know I'm being a good listener?"
YOU'RE SITTING QUIETLY AND LOOKING AT THE TEACHER (Reinforce or correct)
4. "Everybody get ready to *show* me what a good listener does." (Reinforce sitting quietly and looking at the teacher, or correct).

Step 7: CRITERION ROLE PLAY

1. "Let's pretend I am your teacher and I am teaching the class a song. Show me how you would listen while I tell you some of the words. OK class, here are the first words. Everybody listen: 'Puff the Magic Dragon lived by the sea...'" (*Criterion:* Students sit quietly and look at teacher).
2. "Let's pretend your class is in the cafeteria and you've just finished eating lunch. I am the teacher and I'm going around to tables telling students when it's their turn to leave and go out to recess. Show how you would listen so you will know when it's your turn." (*Criterion:* Students sit quietly and look at teacher).
3. "Let's pretend I'm your teacher and our group is having reading now. I'm telling the group how to read a new word. Everyone should be listening, but the person sitting next to you is looking out the window and tapping his/her pencil on the desk like this": (Teacher demonstrates not listening). "You show me what this person *should* be doing to be a good listener." (*Criterion:* Students sit quietly and look at teacher).

Step 8: INFORMAL CONTRACTING

"When a teacher is talking, you be a good listener. A good listener sits quietly and looks at the teacher. What are you going to do to be a good listener?"
SIT QUIETLY AND LOOK AT THE TEACHER (Reinforce or correct).

AREA I: Classroom Skills

SKILL #2: When the Teacher Asks You to do Something

REVIEW: Brief discussion of previous day's skill. Check to see if students followed informal contract.

Step 1: DEFINITION AND GUIDED DISCUSSION

Definition:

"When the teacher asks you to do something you should *do it*. What should you do when the teacher asks you to do something?"
DO IT (Reinforce or correct)
"Let's try these. When the teacher asks you to line up, what should you do?"
LINE UP or DO IT (Reinforce or correct)
"When the teacher asks you to listen, what should you do?"
LISTEN or DO IT (Reinforce or correct)
"When the teacher asks you to put your book away, what should you do?"
PUT THE BOOK AWAY or DO IT (Reinforce or correct)

Guided Discussion:

"Doing what the teacher asks is important for students because it helps them learn. Is it important to do what the teacher asks?"
YES (Reinforce or correct)
"If a teacher asks you to read a word or story and you do it, you're learning to be a better reader. If a teacher asks you to go sit down at your desk and you do it, you're learning to follow directions. If a teacher asks you to take a note home to your parents and bring it back the next day, what should you do?"
DO IT/TAKE IT HOME AND BRING IT BACK THE NEXT DAY (Reinforce or correct)
"If you bring it back the next day, you're learning to be responsible. When the teacher asks you to do something, do it, because it helps you learn."

Step 2: POSITIVE EXAMPLE

Video: One positive example (Debrief: Point out/discuss why example is a positive instance of the skill)

Step 3: NEGATIVE EXAMPLE

Video: One negative example (Debrief: Point out/discuss why example is *not* a positive instance of the skill)

Step 4: REVIEW AND RESTATE DEFINITION

"When the teacher asks you to do something, you should do it. When the teacher tells you to do something, what should you do?"
DO IT/DO WHAT THE TEACHER SAYS (Reinforce or correct)

Step 5: POSITIVE EXAMPLE

Video: One positive example (Debrief: Point out/discuss why example is a positive instance of the skill)

Step 6: ACTIVITIES

Teacher Models:

1. "Let's pretend I'm a student in your class and it's almost time to go to recess. The teacher tells me to put my papers in my desk and go line up. Right away I put my papers in my desk and go line up. That way I'm doing what the teacher says."
2. "Now let's pretend I'm a student in your class working on my math. The teacher looks at the clock and tells me to stop doing math and go right to reading. I stop doing my math and go right to reading. That way I'm doing what the teacher says."

Students Practice:

"This time I want you to tell me how to do what the teacher says."
1. "Let's say you're on the playground. Recess is over and the teacher just blew the whistle. The teacher tells you to line up. What should you do?"
LINE UP (Reinforce or correct)
2. "Let's say some of the students in your class are putting on a play. The teacher is giving instructions, but everyone is talking at once. Your teacher tells everyone to stop talking and listen. What should you do?"
STOP TALKING AND LISTEN (Reinforce or correct)
3. "Let's say it's time to go to P.E., but it's really cold outside. Your teacher tells you to put on your coat. What should you do?"
PUT ON THE COAT (Reinforce or correct)

Step 7: POSITIVE EXAMPLE

Video: One positive example (Debrief: Point out/discuss why example is a positive instance of the skill).

Step 8: CRITERION ROLE PLAY

1. "Let's pretend your teacher tells you to hand in your spelling paper before you go to recess. It's time for recess. What should you do?" (*Criterion:* HAND IN THE PAPER).
2. "Let's pretend you are taking a test. Your teacher tells you to raise your hand if you need to sharpen your pencil. You are working on the test and your pencil breaks. What should you do?" (*Criterion:* RAISE YOUR HAND).
3. "Let's pretend you and your friend are taking a note to the office for the teacher. You and your friend decide to have a race to see who gets to the office first. A teacher steps out of their classroom and sees you running. This teacher tells you to 'walk'. What should you do?" (*Criterion:* Responses which include STOP RUNNING or WALK).

Step 9: INFORMAL CONTRACTING

"When a teacher asks you to do something you should do it. What should you do if your teacher asks you to do something?"
DO IT (Reinforce or correct)

AREA I: Classroom Skills

SKILL #3: Doing Your Best Work

REVIEW: Brief discussion of previous day's skill. Check to see if students followed informal contract.

Step 1: DEFINITION AND GUIDED DISCUSSION

Definition:

"Doing your best work means to follow the directions and write neatly. What does doing your best work mean?"
FOLLOW THE DIRECTIONS AND WRITE NEATLY (Reinforce or correct)
"Let's say this another way. Following the directions and writing neatly is *doing your best work*. Following the directions and writing neatly is called what?"
DOING YOUR BEST WORK (Reinforce or correct)
"Let's try some more. Susie is following the directions and writing neatly. Susie is doing what?"
HER BEST WORK (Reinforce or correct)
"How do we know Susie is doing her best work?"
SHE/SUSIE IS FOLLOWING THE DIRECTIONS AND WRITING NEATLY (Reinforce or correct)

"When you follow the directions and write neatly you are doing your best work. When you follow the directions and write neatly you are doing what?"
YOUR BEST WORK (Reinforce or correct)

Guided Discussion:

"When you do your best work you remember to follow the directions and write neatly. Following directions shows you know what to do and how you're supposed to do it. Writing neatly lets others understand what you have written. Would your teacher like it if you turned in a paper with messy writing that was done wrong?"
NO (Reinforce or correct)
"If you do your best work, your teacher won't have to ask you to do it over again. Do you like doing work over?"
NO (Reinforce or correct)
"Doing your best work makes you feel good about yourself and it shows the teacher you are really trying."

Step 2: POSITIVE EXAMPLE

Video: One positive example (Debrief: Point out/discuss why example is a positive instance of the skill).

Step 3: NEGATIVE EXAMPLE

Video: One negative example (Debrief: Point out/discuss why example is *not* a positive instance of the skill).

Step 4: REVIEW AND RESTATE DEFINITION

"Doing your best work means to follow the directions and write neatly. What does doing your best work mean?"
FOLLOW DIRECTIONS AND WRITE NEATLY (Reinforce or correct)

Step 5: POSITIVE EXAMPLE

Video: One positive example (Debrief: Point out/discuss why example is a positive instance of the skill).

Step 6: ACTIVITIES (Materials: Lined paper, pencils)

Teacher models:

1. "Watch me and I'll show you how to do your best work. Let's say the directions tell me to write 'The cat sat on the hat' on the first line of this paper. I should follow the directions and write neatly, like this": (Teacher writes sentence neatly and shows paper to students).
2. "Now let's say I have to finish doing my best work. The directions are to turn my paper over and write my name on the back." (Teacher turns paper over, writes name, and shows to students).

Students Practice:

"Now I want you to show me how you can do your best work by following my directions and writing neatly." (Before proceeding, *make sure* the following tasks are at an appropriate level. If not, substitute appropriate practice activities as needed).
1. (Hand out papers/pencils) "Everyone get ready to do your best work":
 a. "Write your name at the top of your paper; put your pencil down when you finish." (Reinforce following the directions and an acceptable standard of writing or correct).
 b. "Turn your paper over and write these three letters: A, B, C." (Reinforce following the directions and an acceptable standard of writing or correct).
 c. "Next, write these numbers: 1, 2, 3." (Reinforce following the directions and an acceptable standard of writing or correct).
 d. "Next, write the answer to this question: Is today Saturday?" (Reinforce following the directions and an acceptable standard of writing or correct).

Step 7: CRITERION ROLE PLAYS

1. "Let's pretend the teacher has given us four math problems to do. The directions are to put your name at the top of the paper and finish all of the math problems. Let's say I only finished two of the math problems and wrote my name so messy no one could read it."
 a. "Did I do my best work?"
 b. "What should I have done to do my best work?"
  (*Criterion:*
  a. Students indicate you did not do your best work.
  b. Students indicate that you should have finished the problems/followed the directions and written neatly.)
2. (Materials: Chalk/chalkboard) "Let's pretend we're in the classroom. I'm the teacher and here are my directions. One at a time, go to the chalkboard and write your name. Then go back to your seat and sit down." (Hand first student a piece of chalk). "(*Student's name*), you go first." (*Criterion:* Students follow directions and write name in an acceptable manner).
3. (Materials: Pencils/paper) "Let's pretend we're taking a test. I am the teacher and here are my directions: I want you to write your name and the date at the top of the paper. If you do not know the date, raise your hand and I will help you." (*Criterion:* Students follow directions and write in an acceptable manner).

Step 8: INFORMAL CONTRACTING

"When you have work to do at school you should always follow directions and write neatly. When you have work to do at school, what are you going to do?"
FOLLOW DIRECTIONS AND WRITE NEATLY (Reinforce or correct)

VARIATIONS/ADAPTATIONS

GROUP	ACTIVITY	MATERIALS
Large group, small group or class	• Review rule. Discuss what writing neatly means.	None
Large group, small group or class	• Review rule. Teacher holds up examples of neat work and not neat work and students have to tell if it's neat or not neat and why.	Paper (neat and not neat)

AREA I: Classroom Skills

SKILL #4: Following Classroom Rules

REVIEW: Brief discussion of previous day's skill. Check to see if students followed informal contract.

Note: Teaching this skill is necessarily dependent upon the set of rules applicable to the students' classroom. Before you begin teaching from the script:

(1) Develop a set of classroom rules applicable to the students' classroom.
(2) Prepare positive and negative examples of each rule to model.
(3) Prepare at least three criterion role plays.

Step 1: DEFINITION AND GUIDED DISCUSSION

Definition:

(Before beginning, post classroom rules on the wall or list on chalkboard)
"Following your classroom rules means...."
(Teacher points out each rule listed and goes over each one individually)

Guided Discussion:

"Following classroom rules is important for every student. When everyone follows the rules, it is easier for the teacher to teach and it's easier for you to learn. Following your classroom rules helps everyone get along with each other. How does (select a *classroom rule*) help things go better in your classroom?" (Discuss)
(Repeat for each rule as appropriate)

Step 2: POSITIVE EXAMPLE

a. Teacher models positive instance/correct application of each rule.
b. Debrief: Point out/discuss why each example was positive/correct.

Step 3: NEGATIVE EXAMPLE

a. Teacher models negative instance/incorrect application of each rule.
b. Debrief: Point out/discuss why each example was negative/incorrect.

Step 4: REVIEW AND RESTATE DEFINITION

"Following your classroom rules means...."
(Have students repeat rules orally, reinforce or correct as needed).

Step 5: ACTIVITIES

Teacher models:

(Teacher models both positive and negative examples of each rule. Have students discriminate between the right way and the wrong way, reinforce or correct as needed).

Students practice:

(Teacher calls on students to act out positive examples of each rule, reinforce or correct as needed).

Step 6: CRITERION ROLE PLAYS

(Set up at least three role play situations calling for a demonstration of the classroom rule(s) in the context of the role play. Determine an acceptable standard or criterion for passing the role play).
e.g., "Let's pretend your teacher is working with some students in a reading group. You are sitting at your desk and need to sharpen your pencil. Show me the classroom rule you would follow."
(Criterion: Students raise their hands/or whatever rule is applicable, reinforce or correct as needed).

Step 7: INFORMAL CONTRACTING

"When you are in class you need to follow your classroom rules. Let's say them one more time. What rules are you going to follow?" (Have students repeat each rule)

VARIATIONS/ADAPTATIONS

GROUP	ACTIVITY	MATERIALS
Small group, large group or class	• Review rule. Student(s) are told that they can make up their own rules about school. Teacher lists rules. Teacher reads the first rule and says "The rule is _____, so do what you have to do. (Give examples and nonexamples). "So if you _____, are you following the rule?" (i.e., "The rule is no school on Friday, so if you go to school on Friday are you following the rule?")	Magic marker, tag board or paper
Small group, large group or class	• Review rule. Student(s) make up rules to ball game. Play game, making sure the rules are followed.	Ball
Small group, large group or class	• Review rule. Make up rules for the following situations: Situation 1: On a boat. Situation 2: On a bus. Situation 3: In a hospital. Situation 4: At a swimming pool. Situation 5: On the playground. Situation 6: In the cafeteria. Discuss why rules are important in these situations.	None
Small group, large group or class	• Review rule. You are having five friends over to your house for a party. What rules would you want them to follow in your home?	None

AREA I REVIEW: Classroom Skills

(*Materials needed:* Two pieces of paper and a pencil for each student)

Step 1: RULE REVIEW AND PRACTICE

Rule Review:

"Listening to the teacher means to sit quietly and look at the teacher. Sitting quietly and looking at the teacher is called what?"
LISTENING TO THE TEACHER (Reinforce or correct)

Practice:

"Let's practice listening to the teacher. Sit quietly and look at me while I talk about how you can earn points for using classroom skills every day in your own classroom." (Teacher briefly — for about one minute — reviews classroom incentive program). (Reinforce sitting quietly and looking at the teacher or correct).

Rule Review:

"When the teacher asks you to do something, you should *do it*. What should you do when the teacher asks you to do something?"
DO IT (Reinforce or correct)

Practice:

"Let's try it. Pretend I'm your teacher: 'Class, I would like you to line up quietly at the door'." (Reinforce lining up quietly, or correct).

Rule Review:

"Doing your best work means to follow directions and write neatly. Following directions and writing neatly means what?"
DOING YOUR BEST WORK (Reinforce or correct)

Practice:

(Teacher gives each student a piece of paper and a pencil) "Show me how you do your best work. Write your name on the top line. Skip a line. Write your age. Skip a line. Write your grade in school." (Reinforce writing neatly and following directions or correct).

Rule Review:

"Get ready to tell me the rules of your classroom." (Each student lists the rules in his/her classroom. Reinforce or correct). (Teacher calls on each student to act out a positive instance of one classroom rule). (Reinforce application or correct).

Step 2: ROLE PLAY

1. "Now we're going to practice the classroom skills. Let's pretend you're in your classroom and I'm your teacher. Show me how you would use your classroom skills: 'Class, I'd like you to put away your math books and get ready to listen to instructions'."
"First I'll explain what we're going to do. I'll give you each a piece of paper and a pencil." (Teacher passes out paper and pencils) "We're going to do an experiment to see how well you can follow directions. I'm going to tell you to fold your paper a certain way. Do what I tell you and then wait for more directions" (Note: Teacher may add or omit steps according to students' skill level).
"Fold your paper in half." (Pause) "Fold it in half again." (Pause) "Fold it in half again." (Pause) "Now open up your paper. Trace over all the creases with your pencil. You should have a lot of rectangles on your paper." (Pause) "Now number your rectangles 1, 2, 3, and so on. Put one number in each rectangle."
(Students should have eight rectangles. Reinforce listening to and following directions and writing neatly, or reteach: LISTENING TO THE TEACHER, WHEN THE TEACHER TELLS

YOU TO DO SOMETHING, or DOING YOUR BEST WORK).
2. (Teacher devises role play(s) to test application of students' classroom rules). Example: "You're having trouble with your math worksheet and need some help." (Reinforce raising hand or reteach: RAISE YOUR HAND WHEN YOU WANT TO TALK OR NEED HELP).

AREA II: Basic Interaction Skills

SKILL #1: Eye Contact

NECESSARY PRESKILLS: None

REVIEW: Brief discussion of previous day's skill. Check to see if students followed informal contract.

Step 1: DEFINITION AND GUIDED DISCUSSION

Definition:

"Eye contact means looking into a person's eyes. What does eye contact mean?"
LOOKING INTO A PERSON'S EYES (Reinforce or correct)
"Let's say this another way: Looking into a person's eyes is called *eye contact*. Looking into a person's eyes is called what?"
EYE CONTACT (Reinforce or correct)
"Let's try some more: Tracy is looking into his friend's eyes. Tracy is having what?"
EYE CONTACT (Reinforce or correct)
"How do we know Tracy is having eye contact?"
HE/TRACY IS LOOKING INTO HIS FRIEND'S EYES. (Reinforce or correct)
"When you talk to someone you should be looking into the person's eyes. When you talk to someone you should be having what?"
EYE CONTACT (Reinforce or correct)

Guided Discussion:

"Looking into people's eyes is important. There are two times when you should look into a person's eyes. One time is when you're talking to someone. People like it when you have eye contact when you're talking to them. What's one time when you should look into a person's eyes?"
WHEN YOU ARE TALKING TO A PERSON (Reinforce or correct)
"Another time you should have eye contact is when someone talks to you. When someone is talking to you and you look into that person's eyes, he knows you are paying attention. What's another time when you should look into a person's eyes?"
WHEN SOMEONE IS TALKING TO YOU. (Reinforce or correct)

Step 2: POSITIVE EXAMPLE

"This *is* eye contact." (Teacher looks into student's eyes) "This is eye contact because I'm looking into your eyes."

Step 3: NEGATIVE EXAMPLE

"This is *not* eye contact." (Teacher looks at student's feet while talking). "This is *not* eye contact because I'm *not* looking into your eyes."

Step 4: REVIEW AND RESTATE DEFINITION

"Eye contact means to look into a person's eyes. What does eye contact mean?"
TO LOOK INTO A PERSON'S EYES (Reinforce or correct)

Step 5: ACTIVITIES

Teacher models:

"Watch me and see how I have eye contact with (*student's name*). Let's say you are a new student at school. We are just meeting each other for the first time." (Teacher initiates a conversation by introducing her or himself and asking the student simple questions. Point out to students that you are having eye contact when you are speaking *and* when you are listening).

Students practice:

1. "OK, it's your turn." (Pair off students) "Get ready to practice having eye contact with each other. Start looking into your partner's eyes. Keep having eye contact and tell each other what you did last recess." (Prompt students to begin talking. Reinforce students maintaining eye contact while speaking or listening. Correct as needed).
2. "Let's try another one. Listen. I'm going to have eye contact with some of you in the group. Raise your hand when I'm having eye contact with you." (Reinforce eye contact with the teacher, or correct as needed)
3. (Pair off students) "This time I want you to find out how your partner gets to school in the morning. Show me how you can look into each other's eyes when it's your turn to talk *and* when it's your turn to listen." (Prompt students to begin talking. Reinforce students maintaining eye contact while speaking or listening. Correct as needed).

Step 6: CRITERION ROLE PLAYS

1. "Pretend our scout troop leader is giving us a ride home from an afternoon at the roller skating rink. You and I are sitting in the back seat of the car talking about how much fun we had skating. Show me how you would look at me while we talk." (Give individual turns: Initiate a brief conversation. *Criterion:* Students maintain eye contact while speaking and listening.)
2. (Have students turn away from you) "Pretend we are on the playground. Let's say I walk by you and call out your name. Show me how you would look at me when I call you." (Give individual turns: Call out students' names and initiate a brief conversation. *Criterion:* Students turn around when you call them by name and maintain eye contact while speaking and listening).
3. "Pretend you are all working on your spelling papers in class. Pretend I am your teacher. Show me how you would look at me as I tell you your next assignment." (Explain assignment. *Criterion:* Students maintain eye contact with the teacher).

Step 7: INFORMAL CONTRACTING

"Today when you are talking to your friends or when your friends are talking to you, I want you to remember to have eye contact. What are you going to do when you are talking or listening to your friends?"
HAVE EYE CONTACT (Reinforce or correct)

VARIATIONS/ADAPTATIONS

GROUP	ACTIVITY	MATERIALS
Small group large group Class	• Review definition. Pair students and instruct them to use the masks and look at one another's eyes. Reinforce "looking" behavior. May expand activity to include talking to each other with the masks on while looking at each other's eyes.	Plain paper masks with eye holes cut out
Small group Large group Class	• Review definition. Pair students and instruct them to take turns talking to each other while concentrating on maintaining eye contact. Provide feedback and reinforce group.	None

AREA II: Basic Interaction Skills

SKILL #2: Using the Right Voice

NECESSARY PRESKILLS: Area II, #1

REVIEW: Brief discussion of previous day's skill. Check to see if students followed informal contract.

Step 1: DEFINITION AND GUIDED DISCUSSION

Definition:

"Using the right voice means talk that is not too loud or too soft. What does using the right voice mean?"
TALK THAT IS NOT TOO LOUD OR TOO SOFT (Reinforce or correct)
"Let's say this another way: Talk that is not too loud or too soft is called *using the right voice*. Talk that is not too loud or soft is called what?"
USING THE RIGHT VOICE (Reinforce or correct)
"Stacy was talking to his friend in a voice that was not too loud or too soft. Stacy was using what?"
THE RIGHT VOICE (Reinforce or correct)
"How do we know Stacy was using the right voice?"
HE/STACY WAS NOT TALKING TOO LOUD OR TOO SOFT (Reinforce or correct)
"Annie talked on the phone in a voice that was not too loud or too soft. Annie was using what?"
THE RIGHT VOICE (Reinforce or correct)

Guided Discussion:

"Using the right voice is important when you are talking to people." (Teacher talks softly) "Do you like to listen to people who talk so softly you can hardly hear what they're saying?"
NO (Reinforce or correct)
"Why not?" (Answers indicate that it's hard to hear, etc. Reinforce or discuss) (Teacher talks loudly) "Do you like to talk to people who talk very loudly?"
NO (Reinforce or correct)
"Why not?" (Answer indicates that it makes ears hurt, is uncomfortable, etc. Discuss) "When you talk to someone you should use a voice that is not too loud or too soft. A voice that yells or shouts is too loud. A voice that is very, very quiet is too soft. You need to use a voice that is just right."

Step 2: POSITIVE EXAMPLE

Video: One positive example (Debrief: Point out/discuss why the example is a positive instance of the skill).

Step 3: NEGATIVE EXAMPLE

Video: One negative example (Debrief: Point out/discuss why the example was *not* a positive instance of the skill).

Step 4: REVIEW AND RESTATE DEFINITION

"Talk that is not too loud or too soft is called using the right voice. What is talk that is not too loud or too soft called?"
USING THE RIGHT VOICE (Reinforce or correct)

Step 5: POSITIVE EXAMPLE

"This is using the right voice." (Teacher talks in an appropriate voice ... Not too loud or too soft) "This is using the right voice because it's not too loud or too soft."

Step 6: ACTIVITIES

Teacher models:

"Listen to my voice. Hear how I am talking to you in a nice voice. I am talking loud enough for you to hear me, but I'm not talking so loud that you don't want to listen."

Students practice:

1. "Your turn." (Pair off students) "I want you to practice using the right voice with your partner. Tell each other what your favorite T.V. show is and why you like it." (Prompt mutual conversation, reinforce students using the right voice or correct as needed).
2. "This time I will call on you and you tell me what you would like to be when you grow up by using the right voice." (Give individual turns. Reinforce appropriate voice or correct as needed).
3. (Students need to be seated in a circle). "We are going to practice using the right voice by going around the circle and saying one thing we like about the person sitting next to us. I'll go first." (Teacher begins) "I like (*student name*) because...." (Reinforce students using an appropriate voice, or correct as needed).

Step 7: CRITERION ROLE PLAYS

1. (Pair off students) "Let's pretend you and your partner have gone to buy an ice cream cone after school. I'll be the person who sells the ice cream. Get ready to tell me what kind of ice cream you want." (Teacher role plays a person who works at an ice cream store. Give individual turns asking students what they would like. *Criterion:* Students speak in an appropriate voice).
2. "Let's pretend your class is going to read a play. Let's say each of you gets to be a part in the play. I am the teacher. Get ready to tell me which part you want to be when I call on you." (Teacher gives each student three parts to choose from. Give individual turns, e.g., "Mike you can be a lion, an owl, or a tree. Which part would you like?" *Criterion:* Students speak in an appropriate voice).
3. "Let's pretend your class says the Pledge of Allegiance every morning. I am the teacher. 'OK class, everybody stand up and get ready to say the Pledge of Allegiance'." (Teacher leads Pledge. *Criterion:* Students say Pledge in an appropriate voice).

Step 8: INFORMAL CONTRACTING

"When you are talking to people, you need to use a voice that is not too loud or too soft. Today I want you to practice using the right voice. What are you going to practice today?'
USING THE RIGHT VOICE (Reinforce or correct)

VARIATIONS/ADAPTATIONS

GROUP	ACTIVITY	MATERIALS
Small group, large group or class	• Review definition. Put students in circle and tell what you did yesterday. Use the right voice.	None
Small group, large group or class	• Discrimination Practice: Teacher talks in a voice (the right voice, too loud or too soft). Students raise their hands and tell whether the voice is too loud, too soft or the right voice.	None

AREA II: Basic Interaction Skills

SKILL #3: Starting

NECESSARY PRESKILLS: Area II #1 and #2

REVIEW: Brief discussion of previous day's skill. Check to see if students followed informal contract.

Step 1: DEFINITION AND GUIDED DISCUSSION

Definition:

"Starting means finding someone to talk to. What does starting mean?"
FINDING SOMEONE TO TALK TO (Reinforce or correct)
"Let's say this another way: Finding someone to talk to is called *starting*. Finding someone to talk to is called what?"
STARTING (Reinforce or correct)
"Let's try some more: Sam was on the playground. Sam found someone to talk to. Sam was doing what?"
STARTING (Reinforce or correct)
"How do we know Sam was *starting*?"
HE/SAM FOUND SOMEONE TO TALK TO (Reinforce or correct)

"You are having free time. You find someone to talk to. You are doing what?"
STARTING (Reinforce or correct)

Guided Discussion:

"Starting is the first thing you need to do to make a friend. This is how you start: First, you find a person to talk to. When you start, what do you do first?"
FIND A PERSON TO TALK TO (Reinforce or correct)
"Next, you should look at the person and say something. What should you do next?"
LOOK AT THE PERSON AND SAY SOMETHING (Reinforce or correct)
"Saying hello to a new student in your class is one way of starting. Asking a person what their name is is another way of starting. What are some other ways to start?" (Discuss/suggest examples such as asking the person to play with you, etc.) "Starting is how you get to talk and play with people. How do you get to talk and play with people?"
START(ING) (Reinforce or correct)

Step 2: POSITIVE EXAMPLE

Video: One positive example (Debrief: Point out/discuss why the example is a positive instance of the skill).

Step 3: NEGATIVE EXAMPLE

Video: One negative example (Debrief: Point out/discuss why the example was *not* a positive instance of the skill).

Step 4: REVIEW AND RESTATE DEFINITION

"Finding someone to talk to is called *starting*. Finding someone to talk to is called what?" STARTING (Reinforce or correct)

Step 5: POSITIVE EXAMPLE

Video: One positive example (Debrief: Point out/discuss why the example is a positive instance of the skill).

Step 6: ACTIVITIES

Teacher models:

1. (Select a student to 'start' with. Place the student at a distance). "Watch me and see how I can use starting. Let's say I'm on the playground playing by myself. I see you over there. Pretend I don't know you, but I want to play with you." (Teacher looks around room, sees student, and walks over). "Hi, my name is _____, what's your name? Trading names is one way of starting."
2. (Select another student to 'start' with). "Here's another way to start. Let's say our class is going to lunch and we can choose anyone we want to sit by. Hi (*student's name*), would you sit by me at lunch? That time I *started* by asking (*student's name*) to sit by me at lunch."

Students practice:

1. (Place students around the room) "OK, now you are going to practice starting. Let's say you are all playing by yourselves in the classroom. Pretend you don't know each other. When I say 'start', go find a person to talk to." (Give students the cue to 'start'. Make sure everyone gets a chance to initiate. Prompt different ways of starting, if needed. Reinforce or correct as needed).
2. (Arrange chairs in a row by twos. Pair off students. Seat half the partners in the chairs, leaving an adjacent empty chair for the partner. Have the other students form a line). "OK, let's pretend you are getting on the school bus to ride home. It's the first day of school, so let's say you don't know anyone on your bus. I want this group to get on the school bus and go sit by your partner. Remember, you don't know your partner. Show me how you would use starting." (Reinforce starting or correct. Switch places and have the other half of the group get on the bus).
3. "OK. Now let's pretend you're all at a friend's birthday party. You are just about to sit down in a circle to watch your friend open his/her presents. Get ready to use starting by finding someone and asking that person to sit by you. (Make sure all students have a chance to initiate. Reinforce starting, or correct as needed).
4. (Pair off students) "Let's pretend that every morning you leave your classroom and go to a different teacher for reading. Let's say your reading teacher tells the students in your reading group that everyone gets to leave five minutes early for recess. You go out on the playground and don't see anyone from your regular classroom that you usually play with. Pretend your partner is one of the students in your reading group, but you don't know him/her very well. Let's say you really want someone to play with. Show me how you would 'start'." (Select one of each partner to 'start', then switch. Reinforce starting, or correct).

Step 7: POSITIVE EXAMPLES

Video: Three positive examples. (Debrief: Point out/discuss why examples are positive instances of the skill).

Step 8: CRITERION ROLE PLAYS

1. (Pair off students and arrange them around the room). "Let's pretend your school has just gotten some new rubber balls to play with at recess. Let's say you have been waiting all day to play two-square. It's the last recess of the day and you

want to find someone who will play two-square with you. Find your partner and show me how you would 'start'." (*Criterion:* Students find partners and initiate a conversation which suggests asking the person to play two-square. Set up the situation again, giving the other partner a chance to start).
2. (One-on-one with the teacher) "Let's pretend it's art period at school. You are using the fingerpaints by yourself. Let's say you would like someone to paint with you. I'm a student in your class who is not doing anything. Show me how you would 'start'." (*Criterion:* Student initiates starting which suggests asking if you would like to paint together).
3. (Pair off students) "Let's pretend both you and your partner are new students in the class. The teacher has just told everyone that it's free time. Show me how you would 'start' so you can get to know each other." (*Criterion:* Students initiate starting with each other which includes trading names).

Step 9: INFORMAL CONTRACTING

"Today when you go to recess, I want you to find someone to talk to. What are you dong to do at recess?"
FIND SOMEONE TO TALK TO (Reinforce or correct)

VARIATIONS/ADAPTATIONS

GROUP	ACTIVITY	MATERIALS
Small group, large group or class	• Review rule. Pair students. Tell one half of the students to pretend they are playing in the sandbox and to start playing with their partner. Switch partners. Have the second group pretend they are doing a puzzle.	None
Small group, large group or class	• Review rule. Obtain different animal pictures. Pin an animal picture to a student. Another student will start by going up to the animal, saying hello and asking if they want to do something the animal likes, e.g., "Hello Mr. Kangaroo, do you want to hop through the jungle?" For older students, vary activity by using movie stars' pictures.	Animal pictures Movie star pictures
Small group, large group or class	• Review rule. Give each child the following questionnaire: 1. Find someone with a brother. 2. Find someone with a dog. 3. Find someone with a white house. 4. Find someone with a small car. 5. Find someone whose favorite subject is math.	Questionnaire

VARIATIONS/ADAPTATIONS

GROUP	ACTIVITY	MATERIALS
	Students find answers to the questionnaire by starting with their classmates.	
Small group, large group or class	• Review rule. Pair students. Place an interesting object between the pair. Have one partner "start" a conversation about the object. Put a new object between them and have the other student start an interesting conversation about the object.	Interesting objects

AREA II: Basic Interaction Skills

SKILL #4: Listening

NECESSARY PRESKILLS: Area II #1-3

REVIEW: Brief discussion of previous day's skill. Check to see if students followed informal contract.

Step 1: DEFINITION AND GUIDED DISCUSSION

Definition:

"Listening means to look at the person and pay attention. What does listening mean?"
TO LOOK AT THE PERSON AND PAY ATTENTION (Reinforce or correct)
"Let's say this another way: Looking at the person and paying attention is called *listening*. Looking at the person and paying attention is called what?"
LISTENING (Reinforce or correct)
"Let's try some more: Sandy is looking at her friend and paying attention to what her friend is saying. Sandy is doing what?"
LISTENING (Reinforce or correct)
"How do we know Sandy is listening?"
SHE/SANDY IS LOOKING AT THE FRIEND AND PAYING ATTENTION
"When you look at a friend and pay attention, you are listening. When you look at a friend and pay attention, you are doing what?"
LISTENING (Reinforce or correct)

Guided Discussion:

"Listening to a person shows that you care about what the person has to say. How would you like it if you were talking to someone and that person was looking around like this," (Teacher looks away from students) "and not paying attention?"
WOULDN'T LIKE IT/WOULD THINK HE/SHE WASN'T INTERESTED (Reinforce or correct)
"A good listener looks at the person who is talking and pays attention. Listening helps you make friends because it shows that you want to hear what friends have to say."

Step 2: POSITIVE EXAMPLE

Video: One positive example (Debrief: Point out/discuss why the example is a positive instance of the skill).

Step 3: NEGATIVE EXAMPLE

Video: One negative example (Debrief: Point out/discuss why the example is *not* a positive instance of the skill).

Step 4: REVIEW AND RESTATE DEFINITION

"Looking at the person and paying attention is called *listening*. Looking at the person and paying attention is called what?"
LISTENING (Reinforce or correct)

Step 5: POSITIVE EXAMPLE

Video: One positive example (Debrief: Point out/discuss why the example is a positive instance of the skill).

Step 6: ACTIVITIES

Teacher Models:

"Watch how I listen by looking at one of you and paying attention." (Select a student to model listening with). "(*student name*), tell me what you like to play at recess." (Teacher looks at student and waits for a response). "(*student name*) likes to play _____. I was looking at him/her and paying attention."

Students practice:

1. (Pair off students) "OK. Get ready to show me how you can be good listeners. I want you to take turns listening to your partner tell about what they like to do after school." (Prompt conversations as needed. Reinforce listening attentively or correct).
2. "Now I want everybody to look at me and show me how you can be good listeners. Last Saturday I went to the circus. I saw a funny clown, a lion tamer, and an elephant doing tricks...", etc. "What are some things I saw at the circus?" (Reinforce listening attentively or correct).
3. (Pair off students) "This time I want you to take turns pretending your partner is magic. Your magic partner can give you three wishes. Think of three wishes and tell them to your magic partner. See if your partner was listening by asking them what your three wishes were." (Reinforce listening attentively or correct)

Step 7: POSITIVE EXAMPLE

Video: One positive example (Debrief: Point out/discuss why the example is a positive instance of the skill).

Step 8: CRITERION ROLE PLAYS

1. "Let's pretend that you don't know how to play dodge ball, but a lot of the other kids play it at recess and you want to learn too. Let's say that I am one of the students who always plays and you have just asked me to explain the rules. Show me how you would listen while I tell you the rules." (Role play as if you were a student explaining dodge ball rules. *Criterion*: Students listen attentively).
2. (Pair off students) "Let's pretend you were absent from school yesterday. You just found out that when you were absent, the whole class made a big kite. Let's say your partner helped make the kite. Show me how you would listen while your partner tells you what the kite might have looked like." (Alternate between who tells about the kite and who listens. *Criterion*: Students listen attentively).
3. "Let's pretend it's recess and you're playing on the bars. Let's say I'm a student on the playground who is trying to get a whole bunch of other students together to play tag. Show me how you would listen while I tell when and where we are going to play." (Role play the student who is suggesting the game. *Criterion*: Students listen attentively).

Step 9: INFORMAL CONTRACTING

"Today I want you to be a good listener. What are you going to do today?"
BE A GOOD LISTENER (Reinforce or correct)

VARIATIONS/ADAPTATIONS

GROUP	ACTIVITY	MATERIALS
Small group, large group or class	• Review rule. Students sit in a circle. The teacher says a word. The person on the right repeats the word. This continues until you have gone around the circle.	None
Small group, large group or class	• Review rule. The teacher gives the student(s) a block. The teacher says to touch different body parts with the block as they are named. The students show they are listening by touching the correct body part.	Block

AREA II: Basic Interaction Skills

SKILL #5: Answering

NECESSARY PRESKILLS: Area II #1-4

REVIEW: Brief discussion of previous day's skill. Check to see if students followed informal contract.

Step 1: DEFINITION AND GUIDED DISCUSSION

Definition:

"Answering means saying something after someone talks to you. What does answering mean?"
SAYING SOMETHING AFTER SOMEONE TALKS TO YOU (Reinforce or correct)
"Let's say this another way. Saying something after someone talks to you is called *answering*. Saying something after someone talks to you is called what?"
ANSWERING (Reinforce or correct)
"Let's try some more. Bonnie's friend was talking to her, then Bonnie said something back. Bonnie was doing what?"
ANSWERING (Reinforce or correct)
"How do we know Bonnie was answering?"
SHE/BONNIE SAID SOMETHING BACK (Reinforce or correct)
"After someone talks to you, you should say something back What is that called?"
ANSWERING (Reinforce or correct)

Guided Discussion:

"Answering is what you do right after someone talks to you. What should you do right after someone talks to you?"
ANSWER (Reinforce or correct)
"People like it when you have something to say back. When someone talks to you you should stop, look at the person, and say something back. When someone asks you to sit by them at lunch you should answer. When someone asks you to play a game at recess you should answer. When someone asks you what your name is, what should you do?"
ANSWER/SAY NAME (Reinforce or correct)

Step 2: POSITIVE EXAMPLE

Video: One positive example (Debrief: Point out/discuss why the example is a positive instance of the skill).

Step 3: NEGATIVE EXAMPLE

Video: One negative example (Debrief: Point out/discuss why the example is *not* a positive instance of the skill).

Step 4: REVIEW AND RESTATE DEFINITION

"Saying something after someone talks to you is called answering. Saying something after someone talks is called what?"
ANSWERING (Reinforce or correct)

Step 5: POSITIVE EXAMPLE

Video: One positive example (Debrief: Point out/discuss why the example is a positive instance of the skill).

Step 6: ACTIVITIES

Teacher models:

1. "If you said hello to me and then I said hello to you I would be answering."
2. "If someone asked me to play jump rope and I said 'sure, I'd like to play!' I would be answering."

Students practice:

1. "Let's practice answering. I'll ask you some questions and then you give me an answer." (Give *individual* turns)
   a. "Hi (*student name*), how are you today?"
   b. "(*Student name*) where do you live?"
   c. "I have two brothers and one sister, how many brothers and sisters do you have?"
   d. "What's your favorite TV show?"
   e. "I like to go to the library and check out books on Saturday afternoons, what do you like to do on Saturdays?"
   f. "Do you like pizza? What kind?"
   (Reinforce answering or correct)
2. "Let's say you are walking to the counselor's office. Pretend I'm walking behind you going to the counselor's office too. I come up behind you and say, 'Hello, how are you today?' Tell me some different ways you could *answer* me. (Give individual turns. Reinforce various ways of answering or correct).
3. (Game: Pair off students) "OK. Now you and your partner are going to play a guessing game. This is how to play the game: First, I want you each to pretend you are somebody who works at this school. You could be the nurse, the secretary, a teacher, the principal or whomever you choose. Next, without telling your partner who you are, he/she will start asking questions about you. Each time your partner asks a question, you should answer by telling one thing about the person you are. One partner might say this: 'Do you have long hair?' The other partner might *answer* by saying this: 'No, I have short, curly hair'. (Alternate who gets to answer. Reinforce answering or correct.)

Step 7: POSITIVE EXAMPLES

Video: Two positive examples (Debrief: Point out/discuss why examples are positive instances of the skill).

Step 8: CRITERION ROLE PLAYS

1. "Let's pretend I am a new person just your age who has moved to your neighborhood. Let's say we are waiting for the school bus to come take us to school. Tell me how you would answer as I talk to you." (Give individual turns. Vary the questions accordingly as the conversation progresses). "Hi, my name is ____, what's your name? I live in the yellow house. Where do you live? What grade are you in? Who is your teacher? Maybe we can play together at recess. What do you usually play?" etc. (*Criterion:* Students answer as appropriate)
2. (Pair off students) "Let's pretend we've all just come back to school after summer vacation. Let's say you and your partner are good friends, but you haven't seen each other all summer. Here's the question to ask your partner: 'What did you do over summer vacation?' I will come around and listen to your answers." (*Criterion:* Students answer as appropriate).
3. (Pair off students) "Let's say it's raining really hard outside. It's recess and everybody has to

stay inside the classroom. Pretend you and your partner are trying to decide on a game to play indoors. Ask what your partner would like to play. Others, show me how you would answer." (Alternate who answers. *Criterion:* Students answer as appropriate).

Step 9: INFORMAL CONTRACTING

"Today I want you to be really careful to *answer* after someone talks to you. What are you going to do after someone talks to you?"
ANSWER (Reinforce or correct)

VARIATIONS/ADAPTATIONS

GROUP	ACTIVITY	MATERIALS
Small group or large group	• Review rule. Answering activity: Pair off students or use small groups. Instruct students to ask questions about "favorite things to do." The rule to follow is that a student can't ask another question until they get an answer.	None
Small group or large group	• Review rule. Game: Have one person think of an animal he/she would like to be. The other student asks questions to find out what animal the person is, and the other gives answers with clues, e.g.: a. I'm a big animal. b. Are you a horse? c. No, I am smaller than a horse and have lots of fur. d. Do you have a tail? etc.	None

AREA II: Basic Interaction Skills

SKILL #6: Making Sense

NECESSARY PRESKILLS: Area II #1-5

REVIEW: Brief discussion of previous day's skill. Check to see if students followed informal contract.

Step 1: DEFINITION AND GUIDED DISCUSSION

Definition:

"Making sense means talking about the same things. What does making sense mean?"
TALKING ABOUT THE SAME THINGS (Reinforce or correct)

"Let's say this another way. Talking about the same things is called *making sense*. Talking about the same things is called what?"
MAKING SENSE (Reinforce or correct)
"Nick and Scott are talking about the same things. Nick and Scott are doing what?"
MAKING SENSE (Reinforce or correct)
"How do we know Nick and Scott are making sense?"
THEY/NICK AND SCOTT ARE TALKING ABOUT THE SAME THING (Reinforce or correct)
"When you and your friend talk about the same things you are making sense. When you and your friend talk about the same things you are doing what?"
MAKING SENSE (Reinforce or correct)

Guided Discussion:

"Talking about the same things shows people you are listening. When you listen to what a person is talking about, then you can talk about the same thing. If someone talks to you about recess and you talk about recess too, you are making sense. If someone talked to you about what he had for lunch and you talked about your math worksheet, would you be making sense?"
NO (Reinforce or correct)
"If a friend talked to you about what she did on Saturday and you talked about what you did on Saturday, would you be making sense?"
YES (Reinforce or correct)
"If a group of your friends were talking about a new movie you had just seen, what should you talk to them about?"
THE NEW MOVIE (Reinforce or correct)

Step 2: POSITIVE EXAMPLE

Video: One positive example (Debrief: Point out/discuss why the example is a positive instance of the skill).

Step 3: NEGATIVE EXAMPLE

Video: One negative example (Debrief: Point out/discuss why the example is *not* a positive instance of the skill).

Step 4: REVIEW AND RESTATE DEFINITION

"Making sense means talking about the same thing. What does making sense mean?"
TALKING ABOUT THE SAME THING (Reinforce or correct)

Step 5: POSITIVE EXAMPLE

Video: One positive example (Debrief: Point out/discuss why the example is a positive instance of the skill).

Step 6: ACTIVITIES

Teacher models:

1. "Let's see how to make sense. If you talk to me about what you made during art period and I talk to you about what I made during art period we would be making sense."
2. "Let's say we both went to see the same movie. After it's over we might talk about the parts we both liked best. That way we would be making sense."
3. "If you asked me if I wanted to go get a drink of water and I said 'sure, let's go get a drink,' then we would be making sense."

Students practice:

1. "Let's practice making sense. If I said that 'On Halloween I was dressed up like a ghost,' what could you say to me so we would be making sense?" (Give individual turns. Reinforce making sense about Halloween or correct)
2. "If I said to you that 'I like to play tetherball, or jumprope, or kickball at recess,' what could you say to me so we would be making sense?" (Give individual turns. Reinforce making sense about recess games).
3. (Seat students in a small circle) "Let's see how well we can make sense. I'll start a story and we'll

go around the circle and have everyone add a little part to the story." (Begin a short story, e.g., "Once there was a little boy who lived on a farm. . . ." Give individual turns. Reinforce making sense or correct as needed).

4. (Pair off students) "Pretend your partner is coming over to your house after school. Let's say you are talking about things you would like to do together when you get home. Show me how you would make sense." (Reinforce making sense or correct)

Step 7: CRITERION ROLE PLAYS

1. "Let's pretend you just learned how to tell time and you have a brand new watch on. Someone comes up to you and asks you what time it is. What should you do to make sense?" (*Criterion:* Students suggest telling the person what time it is).

2. "Pretend your whole class goes jogging around the school grounds every day after lunch. Let's say I come running up to you with some new running shoes on and start talking to you like this: 'Hey look, I just got a new pair of shoes!' What are some things you might say to make sense?" (Give individual turns. *Criterion:* Students make sense by saying something about the shoes).

3. "Let's say your class has just come back from a trip to the zoo. Everyone is talking about the animals they saw. Let's say one student says, 'I saw a big lion sleeping in the shade'. What are some things you could say to make sense?" (Give individual turns. *Criterion:* Students make sense by talking about a zoo).

Step 8: INFORMAL CONTRACTING

"Today I want you to make sense when someone talks to you. What are you going to do today?" MAKE SENSE (Reinforce or correct)

VARIATIONS/ADAPTATIONS

GROUP	ACTIVITY	MATERIALS
Small and large group	• Review rule. Teacher puts a different topic on each index card. A student picks an index card and makes sense by talking about the topic on the index card.	Index cards Pen
Small and large group	• Review rule. Students sit in a circle. A student starts talking about a topic. You go around the circle with each student saying something about that topic.	None

AREA II: Basic Interaction Skills

SKILL #7: Taking Turns Talking

NECESSARY PRESKILLS: Area II #1-6

REVIEW: Brief discussion of previous day's skill. Check to see if students followed informal contract.

Step 1: DEFINITION AND GUIDED DISCUSSION

Definition:

"Taking turns talking means you talk, then I talk, then you talk. What does taking turns talking mean?"

YOU TALK, THEN I TALK, THEN YOU TALK (Reinforce or correct)

"Let's say this another way: If you talk, then I talk, then you talk, it is called *taking turns talking*. If you talk, then I talk, then you talk, it is called what?"

TAKING TURNS TALKING (Reinforce or correct)

"Mike talked, then Sharie talked, then Mike talked. Mike and Sharie were doing what?"

TAKING TURNS TALKING

"How do we know Mike and Sharie were taking turns talking?"

MIKE TALKED, THEN SHARIE TALKED, THEN MIKE TALKED (Reinforce or correct)

"If I talk about the school picnic, then you talk about the school picnic, then I talk about the school picnic, we are doing what?"

TAKING TURNS TALKING (Reinforce or correct)

Guided Discussion:

"When you're with a friend, taking turns talking is what you do to share the talking time together. The best way to take turns talking is to talk for the same amount of time you listen to the other person talk. If one person never says anything, are they taking turns talking?"

NO (Reinforce or correct)

"First you talk, then you listen to the other person talk, and when that person is finished, it's your turn to talk again. People take turns talking all the time. If I talk to you about what I did over the weekend, then I should listen while you tell me what you did over the weekend. If you talk to me about a game we are playing, first I listen to you talk, then what should I do?"

TALK ABOUT THE GAME (Reinforce or correct)

Step 2: POSITIVE EXAMPLE

Video: One positive example (Debrief: Point out/discuss why the example is a positive instance of the skill).

Step 3: NEGATIVE EXAMPLE

Video: One negative example (Debrief: Point out/discuss why the example is *not* a positive instance of the skill).

Step 4: REVIEW AND RESTATE DEFINITION

"Taking turns talking means you talk, then I talk, then you talk again. What does taking turns talking mean?"

YOU TALK, THEN I TALK, THEN YOU TALK AGAIN (Reinforce or correct)

Step 5: POSITIVE EXAMPLE

Video: One positive example (Debrief: Point out/discuss why the example is a positive instance of the skill).

Step 6: ACTIVITIES

Teacher models:

1. (Select a student to model with) "Here's one way we might take turns talking: If I could go visit any place in the world, I would go to Disneyland. Where would you like to go?"
(Wait until student responds. Lead further conversation. Conclude conversation, then say:)
"(*Student name*) and I were taking turns talking. First I talked while he/she listened, then he/she talked while I listened."

Students practice:

1a. (Materials: Chalkboard) "If you saw a student at school that you didn't know very well, but wanted to be friends with, what are some things you might take turns talking about if you were meeting this person for the first time?" (Lead students in a discussion about things to talk about if they were just meeting someone. List or draw pictures of the ideas on the chalkboard).

b. (Pair off students) "OK. Let's practice taking turns talking. Pretend your partner is the student you don't know, but want to make friends with. I want you to take turns talking by using the ideas we put on the chalkboard." (Reinforce taking turns talking or correct)

2. (Pair off students) "Let's say your class is planning a Christmas party. I want you and your partner to take turns talking about what the Christmas party will be like." (Prompt conversation as needed. Reinforce taking turns talking or correct).

3. (Game: Pair off students) "I am going to act out a situation. When I finish I want you and your partner to take turns talking about what you think happened." (Teacher role plays a scene by pantomiming all activities, e.g., (a) Playing a baseball game and getting a home run or striking out, (b) A shy student who is meeting someone for the first time, (c) Students getting into a fight about something and then making up. (Reinforce taking turns talking about what happened or correct).

Step 7: POSITIVE EXAMPLES

Video: Three positive examples (Debrief: Point out/discuss why the examples are positive instances of the skill).

Step 8: CRITERION ROLE PLAYS

1. (Pair off students) "Pretend it's recess time, but it's really hot outside. You and your partner decide to go sit in the shade and talk instead of playing a game. Let's say you start talking about things that are nice to do on hot days, like going swimming or drinking lemonade or playing in the sprinklers. Show me how you could take turns talking about things you like to do on hot days." (*Criterion:* Students take turns talking).

2. (Pair off students) "Pretend your whole class is going camping for the weekend in the mountains. Show me how you would take turns talking about things people should bring when they go camping." (*Criterion:* Students take turns talking).

3. (Pair off students) "Let's pretend you could change your name to anything you wanted it to be. Show me how you and your partner would take turns talking about names you might like to have." (*Criterion:* Students take turns talking).

Step 9: INFORMAL CONTRACTING

"Today I want you to take turns talking with someone you like. It could be your teacher, a friend, your mom, or your dad. What are you going to do today?"

TAKE TURNS TALKING (Reinforce or correct)

VARIATIONS/ADAPTATIONS

GROUP	ACTIVITY	MATERIALS
Two students	• Review rule. Teacher selects a topic for students to talk about. Students are told that a timer will be set for listening and talking time. Prompt discussion and set timer for 10-15 seconds. When it goes off, it's the other student's turn to talk for 10-15 seconds. Repeat.	Timer
Group (younger)	• Review rule. Teacher tells students to share with the class something they did over the weekend. Prompt questions. Allow students time to engage in a regular sharing activity.	None

VARIATIONS/ADAPTATIONS

GROUP	ACTIVITY	MATERIALS
Class	• Review rule, Pair students off with one pencil and a piece of paper. Have student draw a person's face by taking turns telling the other person what to draw. EXAMPLE: Student #1 says: This person has a long face (Student #2 draws). Switch roles. Student #2 says: This person has one eye (Student #1 draws).	Pencil/paper

AREA II: Basic Interaction Skills

SKILL #8: A Question

NECESSARY PRESKILLS: Area II #1-7

REVIEW: Brief discussion of previous day's skill. Check to see if students followed informal contract.

Step 1: DEFINITION AND GUIDED DISCUSSION

Definition:

"A question asks for an answer. A question does what?"
ASKS FOR AN ANSWER (Reinforce or correct)
"Let's say this another way: Saying something that asks for an answer is called a *question*. Saying something that asks for an answer is called what?"
A QUESTION (Reinforce or correct)
"Let's try some more: Kathy asked her friends this: 'Where do you play after school?' Kathy asked her friends a what?"
A QUESTION (Reinforce or correct)
"Tom asked his mom this: 'Can I buy my lunch today?' Tom asked his mom a what?"
A QUESTION (Reinforce or correct)

"A question asks for an answer. A question does what?"
ASKS FOR AN ANSWER (Reinforce or correct)

Guided Discussion:

"We ask questions to help us get to know others better and to find out more about them. A good question asks something about another person. If someone just got a haircut, a good question to ask would be, 'When did you get your hair cut?' If someone is absent from school, what would be a good question to ask when the person gets back?"
WHY WERE YOU ABSENT YESTERDAY (or close approximation) (Reinforce or correct)
"If you see someone wearing some shoes you really like, what would be a good question to ask?"
WHERE DID YOU GET YOUR SHOES? (or close approximation) (Reinforce or correct)

Step 2: POSITIVE EXAMPLE

Video: One positive example (Debrief: Point out/discuss why the example is a positive instance of the skill).

Step 3: REVIEW AND RESTATE DEFINITION

"A question asks for an answer. A question does what?"
ASKS FOR AN ANSWER (Reinforce or correct)

Step 4: POSITIVE EXAMPLE

Video: One positive example (Debrief: Point out/discuss why the example is a positive instance of the skill).

Step 5: ACTIVITIES

Teacher models:

1. "Listen to me ask questions. If I say 'What is your name?' that is a question. If I say 'Do you have any pets?' that is a question. If I say 'How old are you?' that is a question. If I say 'Would you like to play hopscotch?' that is a question."

Students practice:

1a. "Your turn to ask questions. Everybody think of some questions to ask me so you can find out more about me." (Give individual turns. Prompt various questions as needed. Reinforce asking questions or correct).
b. (Pair off students) "Now I want you to do the same thing with your partners. Ask questions that will tell you more about your partner." (Reinforce asking questions or correct)
2a. (Materials: Chalkboard) "If a new student just moved to your school, what are some questions you could ask him/her?" (Lead discussion, listing or drawing pictures of types of questions students might ask a new classmate on the board).
b. "Now let's say *you* are the new student at school. What are some questions you could ask your new classmates?" (Lead discussion. List or draw pictures of types of questions a new student might ask his/her classmates on the board).
c. (Pair off students) "Now let's do it. I want you and your partner to pretend that one of you is the new student and one of you is the student who already goes to school here. Use the questions on the board to find out more about each other." (Reinforce asking questions or correct)
3. "Let's pretend your good friend has been absent a whole week. When you come back to school on Monday you see your friend coming to class. Let's say your friend's arm is in a sling. What are some questions you might ask your friend?" (Give individual turns. Reinforce asking questions about what happened, how the person feels, etc., or correct).

Step 6: POSITIVE EXAMPLE

Video: One positive example (Debrief: Point out/discuss why the example is a positive instance of the skill).

Step 7: CRITERION ROLE PLAYS

1. (Pair off students) "Pretend your partner is coming over to your house to spend the night. Pretend this is the first time that your partner has ever stayed overnight. You want to find out things your partner likes to do. I'll come around and listen to the questions you would ask to find out." (Have partners trade parts. *Criterion:* Students ask questions that lead to finding out what the other person likes to do).
2. "Let's pretend you are walking to school and you see one of your classmates walking alone and crying. You think you should see if he/she is OK. What are some questions you might ask?" (Give individual turns. *Criterion:* Students ask questions that suggest finding out if the person is OK, asking if they can help, etc.).
3. "Let's pretend some students you know are in a club at school. You would like to join their club too, but you don't really know anything about it. What are some questions you could ask so you can find out more about joining their club?" (Give individual turns. *Criterion:* Students ask questions that suggest finding out about joining the club, what they do, when they meet, etc.).

Step 8: INFORMAL CONTRACTING

"Today I want you to pick someone you like and ask three questions that will tell you more about that person. What are you going to do today?" ASK SOMEONE I LIKE THREE QUESTIONS (Reinforce or correct)

VARIATIONS/ADAPTATIONS

GROUP	ACTIVITY	MATERIALS
Small group, large group or class	• Review rule. Put an object in a bag. Have students ask questions that will help them identify the object.	Objects
Small group, large group or class	• Review rule. Blindfold a student. Turn him/her around. Have the student get to a precise place by asking question.	Blindfold
Small group, large group or class	• After reviewing the definition, the teacher gives a student an envelope with another student's name on it. The other students guess whose name it is by asking questions, e.g., "Is it a girl?"	Name cards

AREA II: Basic Interaction Skills

SKILL #9: Continuing

NECESSARY PRESKILLS: Area II #1–8

REVIEW: Brief discussion of previous day's skill. Check to see if students followed informal contract.

Step 1: DEFINITION AND GUIDED DISCUSSION

Definition:

"Continuing means keep the talking going. What does continuing mean?"
KEEP THE TALKING GOING (Reinforce or correct)
"Let's say this another way: Keeping the talking going is called *continuing*. Keeping the talking going is called what?"
CONTINUING (Reinforce or correct)
"Let's try some more: JoAnne and Seth kept the talking going. JoAnne and Seth were doing what?"
CONTINUING (Reinforce or correct)
"How do we know JoAnne and Seth were continuing?"
THEY/JOANNE AND SETH KEPT THE TALKING GOING (Reinforce or correct)
"Debbie and Patty keep the talking going. What is it called when Debbie and Patty keep the talking going?"
CONTINUING (Reinforce or correct)

Guided Discussion:

"Continuing means to keep the talking going. We use questions and answers to keep the talking going. What do you call saying something that calls for an answer?"
A QUESTION (Reinforce or correct)
"What do you do when someone asks you a question?"
ANSWER (Reinforce or correct)
"After you start talking to someone or after someone starts to talk to you, you can keep the talking going by asking questions and answering questions together. If someone asks you what your favorite T.V. show is, you can answer and then ask what his/her favorite T.V. show is. If you are talking to someone about things you both like to do,

tell that person what you like to do and then what should you do?"
ASK WHAT HE/SHE LIKES TO DO (Reinforce or correct)
"If you're talking to someone about your families and they ask you how many brothers and sisters you have, what should you do?"
ANSWER/TELL HIM/HER (Reinforce or correct)
"Then what should you do to keep the talking going?"
ASK ABOUT THE OTHER PERSON'S FAMILY (Reinforce or correct)
"As long as you keep the talking going you're continuing. To continue, remember this rule: First *answer*, then *ask*."

Step 2: POSITIVE EXAMPLE

Video: One positive example (Debrief: Point out/discuss why the example is a positive instance of the skill).

Step 3: REVIEW AND RESTATE DEFINITION

"Continuing means keep the talking going. What does continuing mean?"
KEEP THE TALKING GOING (Reinforce or correct)

Step 4: POSITIVE EXAMPLE

Video: Two positive examples (Debrief: Point out/discuss why example is a positive instance of the skill).

Step 5: ACTIVITIES

Teacher models:

1a. "Remember, to keep the talking going you should answer first and then ask. What do you do first?"
ANSWER (Reinforce or correct)
"What do you do next?"
ASK (Reinforce or correct)

b. "Let's see how to use the continuing rule. Let's say we've been playing together on the bars, but we've been getting tired of it. You ask me if I want to go play something else. First, I might *answer* by saying, 'OK, let's play something else'. Next, I might *ask* by saying, 'What else could we play?' If we keep the talking going by *answering* and *asking* more questions, then we are continuing."
2. (Select a student to model continuing with) "Let's see if (*student name*) and I can use the continuing rule...." (Teacher initiates a conversation. Prompt the student using 'answer' and 'ask' as cues, if needed).

Students practice:

1. "Your turn to practice continuing by *answering* first and *asking* next." (Teacher initiates individual conversations with students by leading the interaction with a question. Prompt using 'answer' and 'ask' as cues, if needed. Reinforce keeping the conversation going, or correct).
2. (Pair off students) "I want everyone to think about their favorite subject in school. Think about why you like that subject best. With your partner get ready to keep the talking going by answering and asking questions about your favorite subjects." (Reinforce keeping the talking going, or correct).
3. (Pair off students) "Pretend one of you lives on the beach near the ocean and the other person lives in the mountains. I want you to keep the talking going by answering and asking questions about what it might be like to live where you do." (Reinforce keeping the talking going, or correct).

Step 6: CRITERION ROLE PLAYS

1. (Pair off students) "Let's pretend you and your partner are at a toy store together. Let's say you get to spend the whole day at the toy store playing with all the games and any of the toys you want. Show me how you and your partner can keep the talking going about different things you would do." (*Criterion:* Students answer and ask questions about things to do in a toy store).
2. (Pair off students) "Pretend you and your partner are sitting together in the cafeteria eating

lunch and having a conversation about what you are going to do over the weekend. Show me how you can keep the conversation going about what each other is doing over the weekend." (*Criterion:* Students answer and ask questions about what each other is doing over the weekend.)

3. (Pair off students) "Pretend the *President of the United States* is coming to visit your class. Show me how you and your partner can keep the talking going about things you might like to ask the President." (*Criterion:* Students answer and ask questions about what each other might say to the President).

Step 7: INFORMAL CONTRACTING

"Today when you're at recess I want you to keep the talking going with a friend. What are you going to do at recess?"
KEEP THE TALKING GOING (Reinforce or correct)

VARIATIONS/ADAPTATIONS

GROUP	ACTIVITY	MATERIALS
Small group, large group or class	• Review rule. Topics relevant to students are put in an envelope. A student picks out a topic. A timer is set for one minute and student(s) have to talk about topic until buzzer rings.	Envelope Pens Topic Sentences
Small group, large group or class	• Review rule. Have students sit in a circle. One student starts a story. Go around the circle, with each child adding to the story.	None

AREA II REVIEW: Basic Interaction Skills

Step 1: RULE REVIEW AND PRACTICE

Rule Review:

"Eye contact means to look into a person's eyes. Looking into a person's eyes is called what?"
EYE CONTACT (Reinforce or correct)

Practice:

"Let's do it.
(Teacher talks to student while maintaining eye contact for about ten seconds with only normal digressions — blinking or briefly looking away). (Reinforce or correct)

Rule Review:

"Using the right voice means talk that is not too loud or too soft. Using the right voice means what?"
TALK THAT IS NOT TOO LOUD OR TOO SOFT (Reinforce or correct)

Practice:

"Use the right voice and tell me about what you're going to do after school today." (Reinforce or correct)

Rule Review:

"Starting means finding someone to talk to. Finding someone to talk to is called what?"
STARTING (Reinforce or correct)

Practice:

"Show me how you would use starting with someone in this room." (Reinforce beginning conversation with teacher or another student, or correct).

Rule Review:

"Listening means to look at a person and pay attention. Looking at a person and paying attention is called what?"
LISTENING (Reinforce or correct)

Practice:

"Listen while I talk about some things you can do with friends or on the playground."
(Teacher talks for about 30 seconds). (Reinforce looking at teacher and paying attention, or correct).

Rule Review:

"Answering means saying something after someone talks to you. Saying something after someone talks to you is called what?"
ANSWERING (Reinforce or correct)

Practice:

"Let's see you answer."
(Teacher addresses one or two comments to each student in group). "I hope we have tacos for lunch today (tomorrow). Let's play four square. What would you like to play during recess today? Hi (*student name*). I can't wait until my birthday." (Reinforce or correct answer)

Rule Review:

"Making sense means talking about the same things. Talking about the same things is called what?"
MAKING SENSE (Reinforce or correct)

Practice:

"I'm going to talk about some things and you show me how you would make sense."
(Teacher addresses one statement to each student in group). "I like soccer better than football. I'm saving my money to buy a new bike. Our class went on a field trip to the airport. I'm going to try to get in a basketball game at recess." (Reinforce replies that make sense, or correct)

Rule Review:

"Taking turns talking means you talk, then I talk, then you talk. Taking turns talking means what?"
YOU TALK, THEN I TALK, THEN YOU TALK
(Reinforce or correct)

Practice:

"Let's do it. See how long we can take turns talking about the same thing. I'll start, then everyone will take a turn. There are many things that are fun to do with friends. It's fun to play outside with friends. Some things you can do outside are...."
(Call on student. Give each student in group at least one turn). (Reinforce talking about playing with friends. Prompt or correct as needed)

Rule Review:

"A question asks for an answer. A question does what?"
ASKS FOR AN ANSWER (Reinforce or correct)

Practice:

"I'll say something and you ask me a question about it. Boy, I can't wait until next week! I'm really mad at my brother. My friends and I really had fun at recess today." (Reinforce asking questions or correct)

Rule Review:

"Continuing means to keep the talking going. Keeping the talking going is called what?" CONTINUING (Reinforce or correct)

Practice:

"You can keep the talking going by asking *and* answering questions. If someone asks you a question, you can answer, then ask that person a question. Let's try it."
(Teacher pairs students or works individually with one student) "I'll start by asking a question," (or give one student in pair a question to start with) "and will try to keep the talking going. Remember to make sense. What are we going to do when I come over to your house after school today? I'm new at this school. What do kids do at recess? What are you going to do this Saturday?" (Reinforce answering and asking questions, or correct)

Step 2: ROLE PLAY

"Let's use all of the skills we just talked about. Pretend it's a rainy day and your class is having inside recess. You would like to find someone to talk to. Show me what you would do. (Reinforce initiating conversation with teacher or other student or reteach *starting*. Reinforce or reteach *eye contact, using the right voice,* and *listening*. Reinforce continuing conversation for one or two minutes or reteach *answering, making sense, talking turns talking, a question,* and/or *continuing* as needed). (Repeat for each student in group).

AREA III: Getting Along

SKILL #1: Using Polite Words

REVIEW: Brief discussion of previous day's skill. Check to see if students followed informal contract.

Step 1: DEFINITION AND GUIDED DISCUSSION

Definition:

"Using polite words means saying nice things at the right time. What does using polite words mean?"
SAYING NICE THINGS AT THE RIGHT TIME (Reinforce or correct)
"Let's say this another way. Saying nice things at the right time is called *using polite words*. Saying nice things at the right time is called what?"
USING POLITE WORDS (Reinforce or correct)
"'Please', 'thank-you', 'I'm sorry', and 'excuse me' are polite words. What are some polite words?"
PLEASE, THANK YOU, I'M SORRY or EXCUSE ME (Reinforce or correct)
"Mary borrowed her friend's crayons. Mary told her friend '*thank you*'. Mary was using what?"
POLITE WORDS
"How do we know Mary was using polite words?"
SHE/MARY SAID 'THANK YOU' *or* SHE/MARY SAID A NICE THING AT THE RIGHT TIME (Reinforce or correct)
"Brad said, '*Please* pass the salt'." Brad was using what?"
POLITE WORDS (Reinforce or correct)
"When you say nice things at the right time you are *using polite words*. When you say nice things at the right time you are using what?"
POLITE WORDS (Reinforce or correct)

Guided Discussion:

"Using polite words means you are being kind to other people when you talk to them. When you use words like 'please', 'thank you', 'I'm sorry', and

'excuse me' you are telling people how you feel in a nice way. Do you use polite words when you're talking to people?"
YES/SOMETIMES (Reinforce or discuss)
"When someone does something nice for you and you say 'thank you' you are letting the person know at the right time you like what he/she did. If you are out on the playground and you bump into someone by mistake, polite words to use would be 'excuse me'. What other words could you use?"
I'M SORRY (Reinforce or correct)
"If you needed to borrow a pencil from your neighbor you would say, 'Please may I borrow a pencil?' After he/she gave it to you, what should you say?"
THANK YOU (Reinforce or correct)

Step 2: POSITIVE EXAMPLE

"Watch me and see if I use polite words." (Role play walking by a student and accidentally bumping into their chair) "(*student name*), I'm sorry I bumped into you." (Debrief: Point out/discuss why example was a positive instance of the skill).

Step 3: NEGATIVE EXAMPLE

"Watch and see if I remember to use polite words this time." (Role play previous example, but forgetting to use polite words). (Debrief: Point out/discuss why example is *not* a positive instance of the skill).

Step 4: REVIEW AND RESTATE DEFINITION

"Saying nice things at the right time is called using polite words? Saying nice things at the right time is called what?"
USING POLITE WORDS (Reinforce or correct)
"Polite words are: 'Please', 'thank you', 'I'm sorry', and 'excuse me'. What are some polite words?"
PLEASE, THANK YOU, I'M SORRY, EXCUSE ME (Reinforce or correct)

Step 5: POSITIVE EXAMPLE (Materials: Papers)

(Hand out papers) "Pretend I'm your teacher and everyone has just finished a test: Class, will you *please* hand me your papers?" (Students hand in papers). "Thank you." (Debrief: Point out/discuss why example was a positive instance of the skill).

Step 6: ACTIVITIES

Teacher models:

"Let's listen to me use polite words by saying nice things at the right time."
1. "Let's say I'm trying to find a seat in a dark movie theatre and I accidentally step on somebody's toe. I can use polite words by saying, 'I'm sorry', or 'excuse me'."
2. "Pretend I'm a student in your class working on math. Let's say the person who sits in front of me is talking to their neighbor and I can't do my work because they are talking. I can use polite words by saying, 'Could you please stop talking?' or 'Could you please whisper?' As soon as they lower their voices or stop talking I should say 'thank you'."
3. "Let's say I've just finished eating a big lunch. The person sitting next to me offers me their apple, but I'm too full to eat it. I can use polite words by saying 'no thank you'."

Students practice:

1. "Your turn to practice using polite words. Let's say I'm your teacher and you need to borrow a pencil. What polite word should you use?"
PLEASE (Reinforce or correct)
2. "Let's pretend you came to school and you forgot your reading book. It's time for reading and I tell you that we can share my book. What polite words should you say to me?"
THANK YOU (Reinforce or correct)
3. "Let's say you are chasing after a ball on the playground. You aren't watching where you are going and you accidentally bump into someone. What polite words should you say?"

I'M SORRY or EXCUSE ME (Reinforce or correct)

4. "Let's pretend you are building a sand castle with a group of friends. Another friend comes by and asks you if you want to play basketball. Let's say you don't feel like playing basketball. What polite words could you say to your friend?"
NO THANK YOU (Reinforce or correct)

Step 7: CRITERION ROLE PLAYS

1. "Let's pretend it's raining after school and your friend offers you a ride home. Your mom is already coming to pick you up, so you don't need a ride. Tell me what you would say to your best friend." (*Criterion:* NO THANK YOU).
2. "Let's pretend you are in class sitting at a table drawing with some other students. You get up from the table and bump the arm of the person next to you. Tell me what you would say to that person." (*Criterion:* EXCUSE ME or I'M SORRY).
3. "Pretend you are at the lunch table and you would like someone to pass you the catsup. Tell me which polite word you would use." (*Criterion:* PLEASE).
4. "Let's pretend you just got a new dress/shirt and you're wearing it to school for the first time. I tell you, 'Oh, I really like your new dress/shirt.' Tell me what polite words you would say to me." (*Criterion:* THANK YOU).

Step 8: INFORMAL CONTRACTING

"Today I want you to remember to use polite words at the right time. What are you going to remember to do today?"
USE POLITE WORDS AT THE RIGHT TIME

VARIATIONS/ADAPTATIONS

GROUP	ACTIVITY	MATERIALS
Small group, large group or class	• Review rule. Tell student(s) you are going to describe a situation. They should tell if they would say 'please,' 'thank-you,' 'excuse me' or 'I'm sorry' in the situation.	Situations which call for a response of 'please,' 'thank-you,' 'excuse me' or I'm sorry.'
Small group, large group or class	• Review rule. Tell student(s) you are going to give them a word. They need to describe a situation in which they use the word. (Words: Please, thank you, excuse me, I'm sorry).	None

AREA III: Getting Along

SKILL #2: Sharing

NECESSARY PRESKILLS: Area II #1-9

REVIEW: Brief discussion of previous day's skill. Check to see if students followed informal contract.

Step 1: DEFINITION AND GUIDED DISCUSSION

Definition:

"Sharing means letting someone use something you have. What does sharing mean?"
LETTING SOMEONE USE SOMETHING YOU HAVE (Reinforce or correct)
"Let's say this another way. Letting someone use something you have is called *sharing*. Letting someone use something you have is called what?"
SHARING (Reinforce or correct)
"David was letting Steve use his baseball mitt. David was doing what?"
SHARING (Reinforce or correct)
"I gave Mark half of my sandwich. What was I doing?"
SHARING (Reinforce or correct)
"If you use my pencil while I use your crayons, we are doing what?"
SHARING (Reinforce or correct)

Guided Discussion:

"When you share you use things or enjoy activities with other people. You also take turns. Taking turns on one swing is sharing. Splitting your hamburger is sharing. What do you call it when you give someone a bite of your cookie?"
SHARING (Reinforce or correct)
"If you take turns riding a bike, are you sharing the bike?"
YES (Reinforce or correct)

Step 2: POSITIVE EXAMPLE

Video: One positive example (Debrief: Point out/discuss why the example is a positive instance of the skill).

Step 3: NEGATIVE EXAMPLE

Video: One negative example (Debrief: Point out/discuss why the example is *not* a positive instance of the skill).

Step 4: REVIEW AND RESTATE DEFINITION

"Letting someone use something you have is sharing. Letting someone use something you have is called what?"
SHARING (Reinforce or correct)

Step 5: POSITIVE EXAMPLE

Video: Two positive examples (Debrief: Point out/discuss why the example is a positive instance of the skill).

Step 6: ACTIVITIES

Teacher models:

1. "Here are some ways of sharing: Splitting a candy bar. Taking turns on the bars. Taking turns reading the same book. Letting someone use your scissors. Putting your puzzle together with someone else. Letting a classmate sit at your desk." Etc.
2. "People can share *time* together too, by: Taking a walk together. Taking turns talking. Taking a note to the office together. Eating lunch together." Etc.

Students practice:

1. "What are some other ways of sharing?" (Give

individual turns, continue leading a discussion on different ways of sharing. Reinforce suggestions of ways to share or correct).

2. (Materials: Pencil, paper. Pair off students. Give one partner a piece of paper and the other partner the pencil.) "I want you and your partner to draw a picture. You only have one pencil and one piece of paper. Show me how you might share so you can both help draw the picture." (Reinforce taking turns with pencil and paper, or correct).

3. (Have students form a line) "This time I want you to play follow the leader. Show me how you can work it out so that everybody gets a chance to be the leader for a little while." (Reinforce taking turns who goes first, or correct as needed).

4. "Let's pretend your cat had kittens and you brought them to school for show and tell. Let's say you only brought three kittens, but everybody in the whole class wants to hold and pet them at once. What could you do so that everyone gets a chance to play with the kittens?" (Give individual turns. Reinforce suggestions on how to share: Have students take turns, play with them one at a time, or in groups of three, etc., or correct).

Step 7: CRITERION ROLE PLAYS

1. "Let's pretend you have one piece of gum. I'm your friend and I don't have any gum, but would really like some. How would you share with me?" (*Criterion:* GIVE AWAY HALF or SPLIT IT)

2. "Let's pretend your class just got a computer. Four of you are having free time and want to use the new computer. Ony one person can use it at a time. What could you do to share?" (*Criterion:* TAKE TURNS).

3. "Let's pretend we are friends and we are waiting for the school bus to come pick us up. It starts to rain outside. You have an umbrella, but I don't. What could you do to share?" (*Criterion:* BOTH STAND UNDER THE UMBRELLA).

Step 9: INFORMAL CONTRACTING

"Today in class I want you to share by letting someone use something you have. What are you going to do in class?"
LET SOMEONE USE SOMETHING I HAVE (Reinforce or correct)

VARIATIONS/ADAPTATIONS

GROUP	ACTIVITY	MATERIALS
Small group, large group or class	• Review rule. Pair students. Give one paints and a brush and the other paper. They are to draw a picture together. They have to share in order to do this activity.	Paints, brush, paper
Small group, large group or class	• Review rule. Give each student one color of paper. The paper should be cut in one inch strips. There should be enough strips for the whole class. Each student should have a different color of strips. The students are to make a chain using one strip of each color. They have to share in order to do this activity.	Paper

VARIATIONS/ADAPTATIONS

GROUP	ACTIVITY	MATERIALS
Small group, large group or class	• Review rule. Each student stands with one arm out straight (not bending their elbow) and the other arm behind their back. The teacher puts raisins in each child's hand. The children can eat any raisins that come directly from a hand to a mouth. Remember the child has to keep one hand behind their back and the other hand straight at all times. They will have to share in order to do this activity.	Raisins

AREA III: Getting Along

SKILL #3: Following Rules

NECESSARY PRESKILLS: Area II #1–9

REVIEW: Brief discussion of previous day's skill. Check to see if students followed informal contract.

Step 1: DEFINITION AND GUIDED DISCUSSION

Definition:

"Following rules means everyone plays the game the same way. What does following rules mean?"
EVERYONE PLAYS THE GAME THE SAME WAY (Reinforce or correct)
"Let's say this another way. When everyone plays the game the same way it is called *following the rules*. When everyone plays the game the same way it is called what?"
FOLLOWING THE RULES (Reinforce or correct)
"Cindy and Donna were playing two-square the same way. Cindy and Donna were playing two-square by doing what?"
FOLLOWING THE RULES
"How do we know Cindy and Donna were following the rules?"
THEY/CINDY AND DONNA WERE PLAYING (TWO-SQUARE) THE SAME WAY (Reinforce or correct)
"When you play a game everyone should be playing the game the same way. If everyone plays the game the same way, what is it called?"
FOLLOWING THE RULES (Reinforce or correct)

Guided Discussion:

"We all have to follow rules by playing games the same way so the game can be fun. Have you ever played with someone who wouldn't follow the rules?"
YES or NO
"It's hard to have fun playing when someone doesn't follow the rules. Rules are important because they help the game to be fair and let everyone have a turn to play. Why are rules important?"
THEY HELP THE GAME BE FAIR/LET EVERYONE HAVE A TURN
"Everyone should understand the rules to a game before they start to play. If everyone knows the same rules, everyone can play the game the same way and everyone can have fun."

Step 2: POSITIVE EXAMPLE

Video: One positive example (Debrief: Point out/discuss why the example is a positive instance of the skill).

Step 3: NEGATIVE EXAMPLE

Video: One negative example (Debrief: Point out/discuss why the example is *not* a positive instance of the skill).

Step 4: REVIEW AND RESTATE DEFINITION

"Following rules means everyone plays the game the same way. What does following the rules mean?"
EVERYONE PLAYS THE GAME THE SAME WAY (Reinforce or correct)

Step 5: POSITIVE EXAMPLE

Video: One positive example (Debrief: Point out/discuss why the example is a positive instance of the skill).

Step 6: ACTIVITIES

Teacher models:

1. "Games and activities that students play together have rules to follow so that everyone knows how to play the same way."
   a. "Let's say we are playing jump rope and the rule is: If you step on the rope you have to go out. If I was jumping and then I stepped on the rope, I should *go out.* Let's say you were jumping and then you stepped on the rope. What should you do?"
GO OUT (Reinforce or correct)
"If we keep playing by going out when we are supposed to, we are following the rules."
   b. "Let's say we are playing Old Maid. One rule for playing Old Maid is that we can't look at each other's cards. If I leaned over and looked at your cards, would I be following the rules?"
NO (Reinforce or correct)
   c. "Let's say we are playing tag. One rule is that if someone tags you, you're 'it' and you have to try to tag someone. If everyone plays tag the same way, then we would be following the rules."

Students practice:

1. (Game: Seat students in a circle. Have some sort of small object to pass around) "We are going to play a game and here is the rule: You can only talk when you have the _____. We're going to pass the _____ around the circle and when you have it you can talk. Here's what we are going to talk about: Let's say we could change one thing about ourselves. I want you to tell everyone what you would change about yourself and why." (Teacher begins game, holding object while talking. Pass object to next student. Reinforce following rules or correct).
2. (Pair off students) "This time I want you and your partner to make up your own rules for a guessing game. Then I want you to play the guessing game together by following your rules. I will come around and watch you play." (Prompt student to make up simple rules as needed. As students begin playing, reinforce following the rules, or correct).
3. (Game of your choice, e.g., Seven-up, Duck, Goose, Musical Chairs, etc. Explain rules and begin game. Reinforce students for following the rules or correct as needed).

Step 7: POSITIVE EXAMPLE

Video: Two positive examples (Debrief: Point out/discuss why the examples were positive instances of the skill).

Step 8: CRITERION ROLE PLAYS

1. "Let's pretend your whole class is painting one big picture together. There aren't enough paints for everyone, so the teacher makes a rule that everyone has to take turns and share the paints. Let's say that you've been painting for awhile.

There is someone standing next to you waiting who hasn't had a turn to paint yet. What should you do to follow the teacher's rules?" (*Criterion:* GIVE THEM A TURN or TAKE TURNS)

2. "Let's pretend you are playing four-square. The rule is that if you hit the ball outside the court you have to go out and it's someone else's turn. Let's say you hit the ball out of the court. What should you do?" (*Criterion:* GO OUT)

3. "Let's pretend your class is having team races during P.E. The rule is that you have to stand behind the line and wait for the person to tag you. You see someone who is *not* standing behind the line, so he/she gets a head start."

a. "Is this person following the rules?
b. "What should this person be doing to follow the rules?"
(*Criterion:*
a. NO
b. STANDING BEHIND THE LINE)

Step 9: INFORMAL CONTRACTING

"Following rules means everyone plays the game the same way. When you play a game, follow the rules. What are you going to do when you play a game?"
FOLLOW THE RULES (Reinforce or correct)

VARIATIONS/ADAPTATIONS

GROUP	ACTIVITY	MATERIALS
Small group, large group or class	• Review rule. Student(s) tell rules for different games at school (Four-square, dodge ball, etc.).	None
Small group, large group or class	• Review rule. Student(s) discuss why they have to follow rules.	None

AREA III: Getting Along

SKILL #4: Assisting Others

NECESSARY PRESKILLS: Area II #1-9

REVIEW: Brief discussion of previous day's skill. Check to see if students followed informal contract.

Step 1: DEFINITION AND GUIDED DISCUSSION

Definition:

"Assisting others means doing nice things for others when they need help. What does assisting others mean?"
DOING NICE THINGS FOR OTHERS WHEN THEY NEED HELP (Reinforce or correct)
"Let's say this another way. Doing nice things for others when they need help is called *assisting others*. Doing nice things for others when they need help is called what?"
ASSISTING OTHERS (Reinforce or correct)
"Let's try some more. Karen did a nice thing for her friend when she needed help. Karen was doing what?"
ASSISTING HER FRIEND or ASSISTING OTHERS (Reinforce or correct)
"How do we know Karen was assisting others?"
SHE/KAREN DID A NICE THING FOR HER FRIEND WHEN SHE NEEDED HELP. (Reinforce or correct)

"Tim helped Blake and Peter carry a table. Tim was doing what?"
ASSISTING OTHERS or ASSISTING BLAKE AND PETER (Reinforce or correct)
"Shawn fell down. Carrie helped Shawn stand up. Carrie was doing what?"
ASSISTING OTHERS or ASSISTING SHAWN (Reinforce or correct)

Guided Discussion:

"When someone looks like he or she needs help, a nice thing to do is to go over and ask if you can help. Helping someone shows that you care about that person. If you spilled your crayons on the floor, I would go over and ask if you wanted help picking them up. If you said 'yes', what should I do?"
HELP PICK THEM UP (Reinforce or correct)
"Another time to help is when someone gets hurt. If you fell down at recess and hurt yourself, I would go over and ask if you needed help. If you said, 'yes', what should I do?"
HELP ME GET UP/GET A BANDAID/TAKE ME TO THE NURSE (Reinforce or correct)

Step 2: POSITIVE EXAMPLE

Video: One positive example (Debrief: Point out/discuss why the example is a positive instance of the skill).

Step 3: NEGATIVE EXAMPLE

Video: One negative example (Debrief: Point out/discuss why the example is *not* a positive instance of the skill).

Step 4: REVIEW AND RESTATE DEFINITION

"Assisting others means doing nice things for others when they need help. What does assisting others mean?"
DOING NICE THINGS FOR OTHERS WHEN THEY NEED HELP (Reinforce or correct)

Step 5: POSITIVE EXAMPLE

Video: Three positive examples (Debrief: Point out/discuss why the example is a positive instance of the skill).

Step 6: ACTIVITIES

Teacher models:

1. "Here are some ways of assisting others":
a. "Let's say (*student name*) is passing out papers and he/she drops them all over the floor. First I would go over and ask if I could help. If _____ says yes, I would help him/her pick the papers up."
b. "If (*student name*) falls down and scrapes his/her arm, the *first* thing I would do is go over and ask (*student name*) if he/she needs help. Next, I would help him/her stand up."
c. "If you see someone who needs help, what should you do first?"
ASK IF THE PERSON NEEDS HELP or ASK IF YOU CAN HELP (Reinforce or correct)
"If that person *does* need help, what should you do next?"
HELP (Reinforce or correct)
d. "What are some different ways of assisting others?" (Lead students in a discussion about different ways of helping others. Briefly roleplay student's suggestions, as appropriate).

Students practice:

1. (Pair off students) "Now I want you to show me how you can assist others."
a. "Pretend your partner is carrying their tray to the lunch table in the cafeteria. Pretend your partner trips and falls and their tray spills all over. Show me some things you could do to help." (Have students role play each part. Reinforce suggestions to ask if help is needed, help clean up, help the person up, get another tray, etc., or correct as needed).
b. "Pretend you see someone on the playground get hit by a ball. You see that the person's nose is starting to bleed. What are some things you

could do to help?" (Give individual turns. Reinforce suggestions to ask if help is needed, go get a kleenex, get a teacher, or take student to the nurse, etc., or correct).

c. "Pretend you've come to school early one morning. You see your teacher walking toward the classroom carrying a whole bunch of books. What are some things you could do to help the teacher?" (Give individual turns. Reinforce suggestions to ask if help is needed, help carry the books, open the door, etc., or correct as needed).

Step 7: CRITERION ROLE PLAYS

1. "Pretend you have a friend who gets around in a wheelchair because she can't walk. Pretend your friend is wheeling herself down the hallway to class. Let's say you see that your friend's wheelchair gets stuck and she can't go any further."
  a. "What should you do first?"
  b. "If your friend does need help, what could you do next?"
(Criterion:
a. ASK IF HELP IS NEEDED

b. Accept responses which suggest pushing the person to class, helping them get started, etc.).

2. "Pretend I'm your P.E. teacher. We are all going out to the field to play softball. I am carrying the bag of softball equipment and it's very heavy." (Teacher role plays carrying a heavy bag). "Show me what you would do to help." (Criterion: Students ask if help is needed, students help carry the bag).

3. (Pair off students) "Pretend you and your partner are roller skating together. Let's say one of you is skating too fast and you bump into each other. You both fall down. Show me how you would help each other." (Criterion: Students ask each other if help is needed, help each other stand up).

Step 8: INFORMAL CONTRACTING

"Next time you see someone who needs help, I want you to go over and see if there's anything you can do to help. Next time you see someone who needs help what are you going to do?"
SEE IF I CAN HELP (Reinforce or correct)

VARIATIONS/ADAPTATIONS

GROUP	ACTIVITY	MATERIALS
Small group, large group or class	• Review rule. Student(s) are told the following situations. They discuss how they could assist others. *Situation 1:* Someone has too much to carry. *Situation 2:* Someone has to clean up her room *Situation 3:* Someone has lost his pencil. *Situation 4:* Someone is new at school. She doesn't know her way around.	None
Small group, large group or class	• Review rule. Each student tells a situation in which they have assisted others.	None

AREA III: Getting Along

SKILL #5: Touching the Right Way

NECESSARY PRESKILLS: Area II #1-9

REVIEW: Brief discussion of previous day's skill. Check to see if students followed informal contract.

Step 1: DEFINITION AND GUIDED DISCUSSION

Definition:

"Touching the right way means not touching too long or too hard. What does touching the right way mean?"
NOT TOUCHING TOO LONG OR TOO HARD (Reinforce or correct)
"Let's say this another way. Not touching too long or too hard is called *touching the right way*. Not touching too long or too hard is called what?"
TOUCHING THE RIGHT WAY (Reinforce or correct)
"Jake did not touch his friend too long or too hard. Jake was doing what?"
TOUCHING THE RIGHT WAY (Reinforce or correct)
"How do we know Jake was touching the right way?"
HE/JAKE DID NOT TOUCH TOO LONG OR TOO HARD
"Betsy tapped her friend on the shoulder. Betsy did not touch too long or too hard. Betsy was doing what?"
TOUCHING THE RIGHT WAY (Reinforce or correct)

Guided Discussion:

"Touching a person the right way at the right times is one special way of showing you care. An important thing to remember is not to touch too long a time or touch too hard. What does it feel like if someone touches you too hard?"
IT HURTS (Reinforce or correct)
"Touching too long makes people feel uncomfortable and touching too hard hurts. We don't use touching all the time, but there are some times when touching is OK. When you see someone who has been hurt falling down you can touch the right way by helping the person up. What is doing nice things for others when they need help called?"
ASSISTING OTHERS (Reinforce or correct)
"When you need to get someone's attention you can touch the right way by tapping him or her lightly. What's another time touching is OK?"
WHEN YOU WANT TO GET SOMEONE'S ATTENTION (Reinforce or correct)
"When someone does something you like you can let the person know he or she did a good job by giving them a pat on the back. If someone on your team scored a soccer goal, what could you do to show you liked what he or she did?"
PAT HIM ON THE BACK (Reinforce or correct)

Step 2: POSITIVE EXAMPLE

(Teacher models positive example) "Watch and see how I touch you the *right* way when you hit a home run."
(Teacher pats student on back and says, "Great hit!") (Debrief: Point out/discuss why the example is a positive instance of the skill).

Step 3: NEGATIVE EXAMPLE

(Teacher models negative example) "Watch and see if I touch the right way this time."
(Teacher tugs on a student's shirt) (Debrief: Point out/discuss why the example is *not* a positive instance of the skill).

Step 4: REVIEW AND RESTATE DEFINITION

"Touching the right way means not touching too long or too hard. What does touching the right way mean?"

NOT TOUCHING TOO LONG OR TOO HARD
(Reinforce or correct)

Step 5: POSITIVE EXAMPLE

(Teacher models positive example: Have a student sit on the floor) "If I saw that you fall down I could touch you the right way by helping you up like this."
(Teacher helps student stand up) (Debrief: Point out/discuss why the example is a positive instance of the skill).

Step 6: ACTIVITIES

Teacher models:

1. "Here are some ways of touching the right way":
   a. (Model with a student) "If I want to get (*student's name*) attention, I could touch the right way by tapping him/her lightly, like this": (Tap student) "Was I touching too long or too hard?" NO (Reinforce or correct)
   b. (Model with a student) "If (*student's name*) did something I liked, I could touch the right way by giving him/her a pat on the back, like this": (Pat student on back) "Great job! Was I touching too long or too hard?" NO (Reinforce or correct)

Students practice:

1. "First I want you to tell me if what I do is touching the right way or the wrong way." (Select a student to model with. Alternate between touching a student the right way or the wrong way and ask students to discriminate, e.g., "Was that touching the right way? Why?" or "Why not?"
2. (Pair off students) "Take turns having each other sit on the floor as if you fell down. Practice touching the right way by helping each other up." (Reinforce helping up appropriately or correct)
3. (Pair off students) "Pretend you have been teaching your partner how to shoot baskets. Your partner has been practicing every recess, but just can't seem to make a basket. It's the last recess of the day and all of a sudden your partner makes his/her first basket! Show me how you could touch the right way to let your partner know that you're glad he/she made a basket." (Have students role play each part. Reinforce a pat or correct)

Step 7: CRITERION ROLE PLAY

1. (Form students in a line. Teacher is line leader). "Let's pretend our class is standing in line waiting for our teacher to come take us in from recess. Let's say the teacher comes and tells us to start walking, but the person in front of you doesn't hear the teacher. Show me how you would touch the person in front of you the right way to let him/her know it's time to go in." (*Criterion:* Students tap person in front of them lightly).
2. (Pair off students) "Pretend you were walking across the classroom with some paint and you dropped it on the floor. You went to get some paper towels, but on your way back to clean up the paint you saw that one of your classmates had slipped on the paint and fallen down. Take turns showing me how you would touch the right way if this happened." (*Criterion:* Students help each other up appropriately).
3. (Pair off students) "Let's pretend you're playing soccer and your friend who is the goalie blocks a kick. Show me how you would touch the right way to let your friend know he or she did a good job." (*Criterion:* Students give a pat on the back).

Step 8: INFORMAL CONTRACTING

"Touching the right way means not touching too long or too hard. When you touch someone you need to do it *the right way*. When you touch someone the right way what are you going to do?" NOT TOUCH TOO LONG OR TOO HARD (Reinforce or correct)

VARIATIONS/ADAPTATIONS

GROUP	ACTIVITY	MATERIALS
Small group	• Review rule. Teacher prepares 5-6 situational cards that call for touching, e.g., when someone falls down, when you need to get someone's attention, etc. AND 5-6 separate answer cards that tell what you do, e.g., help them up, pat on the back, etc. Give one set of cards to each student. Give a signal and have each student place a card on the table at the same time. Have students decide if the situation and answer cards match. E.G., SITUATION: When someone falls down. ANSWER: Shake hands. If not, act out or have them discuss correct answer. Shuffle cards. Repeat.	Pre-prepared 4×5 situational/answer cards
Small group, large group or class	• Review rule. Discrimination training activity: demonstrate touching the right way/wrong way. Have students tell you if it is right/wrong way and why.	None
Small group, large group or class	• Review rule. Student(s) have to tell or show the right way to touch in the following situations: *Situation 1:* Patting a cat. *Situation 2:* Shaking hands. *Situation 3:* A pat on the back. *Situation 4:* "Give me five." *Situation 5:* A hug. *Situation 6:* Holding a baby.	None

AREA III REVIEW: Getting Along Skills

Step 1: RULE REVIEW AND PRACTICE

Rule Review:

"Using polite words means saying nice things at the right time. Saying nice things at the right time is what?"
USING POLITE WORDS (Reinforce or correct)
"'Please', 'thank you', and 'excuse me' are examples of polite words. What are some polite words?"
PLEASE, THANK YOU, EXCUSE ME (Reinforce or correct)

Practice:

"Let's practice using polite words. Pretend your hands are very sticky. Show me how you would ask a friend politely to open the door for you."
PLEASE OPEN THE DOOR FOR ME
"What would you say after your friend opened the door for you?"
THANK YOU
"Pretend you weren't looking where you were going and bumped into someone. What would you say?"
EXCUSE ME/I'M SORRY (Reinforce responses or correct)

Rule Review:

"Letting someone use something you have is sharing. Letting someone use something you have is what?"
SHARING (Reinforce or correct)

Practice:

"Let's do it. Pretend you and a friend are walking home from school together. You have a candy bar, but your friend doesn't. Show me how you would share." (Reinforce sharing candy bar or correct)

Rule Review:

"Following rules means everyone plays the game the same way. When everyone plays the game the same way it is called what?"
FOLLOWING RULES (Reinforce or correct)

Practice:

"Pretend you're playing bar tag. The rules are if you touch the ground or get tagged, you're 'it'. Pretend you slip off the bars and touch the ground. What should you do?"
SAY "I'M IT" (Reinforce following rules or correct)

Rule Review:

"Doing nice things for others when they need help is assisting others. What is doing nice things for others when they need help?"
ASSISTING OTHERS (Reinforce or correct)

Practice:

"Let's pretend you see a friend trying to move a heavy box. Show me what you would do." (Reinforce helping friend or correct)

Rule Review:

"Touching the right way means not touching too long or too hard. What does touching the right way mean?"
NOT TOUCHING TOO LONG OR TOO HARD (Reinforce or correct)

Practice:

"Let's do it. Show me how you would touch me to get my attention. Show me how you would touch me to let me know you like the goal I kicked in our soccer game. Show me how you would touch the right way if I fell down while we were roller skating." (Reinforce a tap on the shoulder, pat on the back, and helping up, or correct)

Step 2: ROLE PLAY

1a. "Let's practice all the getting along skills. Pretend you get out to recess early and you start shooting baskets. Soon a friend of yours comes out to watch and looks like he/she would like to shoot, too. Show me what you would do."

b. "Your friend suggests you play one-on-one. The rules are if someone calls a foul you have to give up the ball. Your friend calls a foul on you. Show me what you would do."

c. "While you're playing, you run into your friend pretty hard and knock him/her down. Show me what you would do."

(Reinforce giving friend a turn or reteach *sharing*; reinforce giving up the ball or reteach *following rules*; reinforce saying "I'm sorry" or reteach *using polite words*).

2a. "Here's another chance to use all of the getting along skills. Let's say you're swinging on a big tire swing on the playground. A girl from your class is waiting for a turn. The swing is big enough for two or three people. Show me what you would do."

b. "You and your friend swing for awhile and some more kids come to wait for a turn. One of the kids in line starts pushing you. What would you say to show you like what he/she is doing?"

c. "The rule on the playground is that when people are waiting to swing, turns can only last three minutes. You and your friend have been swinging three minutes. What should you do?"

d. "The kids who get on the swing after you are having a hard time getting started. What would you do?"

e. "The kids swing for three minutes and you want to tell them time is up, but you can't seem to get their attention. Show me how you would touch one of them to get his/her attention."

(Students demonstrate *sharing, using polite words, following rules, assisting others* and *touching the right way*). (Reinforce getting along skills or correct)

AREA IV: Making Friends

SKILL #1: Good Grooming

NECESSARY PRESKILLS: Area II #1-9

REVIEW: Brief discussion of previous day's skill. Check to see if students followed informal contract.

Step 1: DEFINITION AND GUIDED DISCUSSION

Definition:

"Good grooming means being neat and clean. What does good grooming mean?"
BEING NEAT AND CLEAN (Reinforce or correct)

"Let's say this another way: Being neat and clean is called *good grooming*. Being neat and clean is called what?"
GOOD GROOMING (Reinforce or correct)
"Jane is neat and clean. Jane is using what?"
GOOD GROOMING (Reinforce or correct)
"How do I know Jane is using *good grooming*?"
SHE/JANE IS NEAT AND CLEAN (Reinforce or correct)
"Being neat and clean is called *good grooming*. Being neat and clean is called what?"
GOOD GROOMING (Reinforce or correct)

Guided Discussion:

"Good grooming is important because it shows others that you care about yourself. People like to spend time with friends who look clean and neat. You can look good by wearing clean clothes and by

wearing your clothes the right way. What's one way to look good?"
WEAR CLEAN CLOTHES/WEAR YOUR CLOTHES THE RIGHT WAY (Reinforce or correct)
"You wear your clothes the right way when you wear clothes that fit, when you zip up your zipper, button your buttons and tie your shoes. Good grooming also means making sure your teeth are brushed and your hair is combed and that you take a bath or shower. What's one other way to look good?"
BRUSH YOUR TEETH/COMB YOUR HAIR/TAKE A BATH OR SHOWER (Reinforce or correct)

Step 2: POSITIVE EXAMPLE

Video: One positive example (Debrief: Point out/discuss why the example is a positive instance of the skill).

Step 3: NEGATIVE EXAMPLE

Video: One negative example (Debrief: Point out/discuss why the example is *not* a positive instance of the skill).

Step 4: REVIEW AND RESTATE DEFINITION

"Good grooming means being neat and clean. What does good grooming mean?"
BEING NEAT AND CLEAN (Reinforce or correct)

Step 5: POSITIVE EXAMPLE

(Teacher models) "It was really windy at recess. When I got back to my class, my shirt was untucked and my hair was a mess. I tucked in my shirt and combed my hair." (Debrief: Point out/discuss why the example is a positive instance of the skill).

Step 6: ACTIVITIES

Teacher models:

1. "Here's what I need to do to be well-groomed: I comb and brush my hair; I wash my hands and face; I brush my teeth; and tonight I'll take a bath." (Teacher role plays each activity).

Students practice:

1. "Pretend you had pizza for lunch and got your hands and face messy. Show me what you would do before going out to recess." (Reinforce washing hands and face or correct).
2. "Let's say you played very hard at recess and your clothes got messed up. Your shirt tail came out, your shoes are untied. Show me what you would do to look neat again." (Reinforce tucking in shirt, tying shoes, or correct).
3. "It was stormy when you came to school and your hair got messed up in the wind and rain. Show me what you would do before going to your classroom so you would be well-groomed."(Reinforce combing and brushing hair or correct).

Step 7: CRITERION ROLE PLAYS

1. "Let's pretend you are getting dressed for school. Show me some of the things you should do so you will look neat and clean." (*Criterion:* Brush hair/teeth; wash, comb hair, etc.).
2. "Let's pretend you're out at recess and you get a little dirty playing dodge ball so you go to the bathroom to clean up. Show me what good grooming things you would do." (*Criterion:* Wash hands/face, comb hair, check clothes, etc.).
3. "Let's pretend you're going to a friend's house after school and you want to look neat and clean. What should you check when you look in the mirror?" (*Criterion:* Hair combed, face and hands clean, clothes buttoned and zipped, shirt tucked in, shoes tied, etc., or correct).

Step 8: INFORMAL CONTRACTING

"Tomorrow before school I want you to use good grooming. What are you going to do before school tomorrow?"
USE GOOD GROOMING (Reinforce or correct)

VARIATIONS/ADAPTATIONS

GROUP	ACTIVITY	MATERIALS
Small group, large group or class	• Review rule. Each student tells their schedule for good grooming.	None
Small group, large group or class	• Review rule. Students are shown pictures of people who are messy. Students have to tell how they can look good by using good grooming.	Pictures of messy people

AREA IV: Making Friends

SKILL #2: Smiling

NECESSARY PRESKILLS: Area II #1-9

REVIEW: Brief discussion of previous day's skill. Check to see if students followed informal contract.

Step 1: DEFINITION AND GUIDED DISCUSSION

Definition:

"Smiling shows you like someone or are having fun. Smiling shows what?"
YOU LIKE SOMEONE OR ARE HAVING FUN (Reinforce or correct)
"Let's say this another way: When you like someone or are having fun you can show it by smiling. When you like someone or are having fun you can show it by doing what?"
SMILING (Reinforce or correct)
"Let's try some more: Ted really likes his friend. Ted can show his friend that he really likes him by doing what?"
SMILING
"Jenifer and Jeanie are having fun together. Jenifer and Jeanie can show each other they are having fun by doing what?"
SMILING (Reinforce or correct)
"Smiling shows your friends that you like them. What does smiling show your friends?"
THAT YOU LIKE THEM (Reinforce or correct)
"Smiling also shows your friends that you are having fun. Smiling also shows your friends that you are having what?"
FUN (Reinforce or correct)

Guided Discussion:

"Everyone knows what a smile is. Let me see you smile." (Students smile) "When you see friends who are having fun together they smile at each other a lot. Would you rather spend time with someone who was smiling or someone who looked grouchy?"
SOMEONE WHO IS SMILING (Reinforce or correct)
"When you smile at other children it makes them happy and they might like to be your friend."

Step 2: POSITIVE EXAMPLE

Video: One positive example (Debrief: Point out/discuss why the example is a positive instance of the skill).

Step 3: NEGATIVE EXAMPLE

Video: One negative example (Debrief: Point out/discuss why the example is *not* a positive instance of the skill).

Step 4: REVIEW AND RESTATE DEFINITION

"Smiling shows you like someone or are having fun. Smiling shows what?"
YOU LIKE SOMEONE OR ARE HAVING FUN
(Reinforce or correct)

Step 5: POSITIVE EXAMPLE

(Teacher models smiling) "(*student name*), I like being friends with you!" (Debrief: Point out/discuss why the example is a positive instance of the skill).

Step 6: ACTIVITIES

Teacher models:

1a. "Watch me again. Let's say we are all friends and you just asked me to play with you at recess. I would smile at you and say, 'Sure!'" (Teacher smiles)
b. "Let's say we have been having a great time swimming together all afternoon. I want to let you know that I like you and that this has been a great day. I could do that by smiling at you like this:" (Teacher smiles).

Students practice:

1. "Let's pretend it's a cold afternoon and you are going to your friend's house after school. You and your friend go into the kitchen and he/she surprises you with a cup of hot chocolate. Show me how you could show your friend you're happy *without* talking." (Reinforce smiling or correct).
2. "Let's pretend you're at the park taking a walk. Someone just your age walks by and smiles at you. Show me how you would look at that person." (Reinforce smiling or correct).
3. (Have students sit in a small group) "Pretend you are with a group of your friends having an ice cream cone after school. Everyone is having a good time together. Show each other that you are having fun." (Reinforce smiling at each other or correct).

Step 7: CRITERION ROLE PLAYS

1. "Let's say you just got on the school bus and someone you like comes to sit next to you. Show me how you would look at your friend to let him/her know you're glad he's/she's sitting with you." (*Criterion:* Smile)
2. (Pair off students) "Let's pretend you and your partner are on the same softball team. One of you just hit a home run so your team won the game! How would you show each other that it's been a great game and you're having fun?" (*Criterion:* Students smile at each other).
3. (Pair off students) "Let's pretend it's the first day of school. Pretend you and your partner are good friends from last year, but you haven't seen each other all summer. Show me how you would look at each other to show that you are happy to meet again." (*Criterion:* Students smile at each other).

Step 8: INFORMAL CONTRACTING

"Today I want you to try something fun. Think about smiling. When you see somebody walking by you at recess or in the cafeteria, try smiling at them and see what happens. What are you going to do today?"
SMILE (Reinforce or correct)

VARIATIONS/ADAPTATIONS

GROUP	ACTIVITY	MATERIALS
Small group, large group or class	• Review rule. Student(s) have to tell if they would smile in the following situations: *Situation 1:* When they get 100% on a paper. *Situation 2:* When someone falls down and is hurt. *Situation 3:* When someone tells you a joke. *Situation 4:* When you're watching a funny movie. *Situation 5:* When someone is crying. *Situation 6:* When someone brings you a surprise.	None
Small group, large group or class	• Review rule. Students tell situations that make them smile.	None

AREA IV: Making Friends

SKILL #3: Complimenting

NECESSARY PRESKILLS: Area II #1-9

REVIEW: Brief discussion of previous day's skill. Check to see if students followed informal contract.

Step 1: DEFINITION AND GUIDED DISCUSSION

Definition:

"Complimenting means saying what you like about a person. What does complimenting mean?"
SAYING WHAT YOU LIKE ABOUT A PERSON (Reinforce or correct)
"Let's say this another way: Saying what you like about a person is called *complimenting*. Saying what you like about a person is called what?"
COMPLIMENTING (Reinforce or correct)
"Audrey said something she liked about her friend. Audrey was doing what?"
COMPLIMENTING (Reinforce or correct)
"How do we know Audrey was complimenting her friend?"
SHE/AUDREY SAID SOMETHING SHE LIKED ABOUT HER FRIEND (Reinforce or correct)
"When you say what you like about a friend, you are giving a compliment. When you say what you like about a friend, you are giving a what?"
A COMPLIMENT (Reinforce or correct)

Guided Discussion:

"Complimenting is a special way of telling a person what you like about him/her. You can give compliments when someone does something to help you or when someone does something you like. What's one time to give a compliment?"
WHEN SOMEONE HELPS YOU/WHEN SOMEONE DOES SOMETHING YOU LIKE (Reinforce or correct)
"People like to be complimented because it makes them feel good. If your teacher gives you a compliment like: 'Good job *(student name)*,' how does that make you feel?"
GOOD (Reinforce or correct)
"If someone invited you to play you could say, 'That was really nice of you to ask me to play.'

What do you call it when you tell someone you like what they did?"
A COMPLIMENT (Reinforce or correct)

Step 2: POSITIVE EXAMPLE

Video: One positive example (Debrief: Point out/discuss why the example is a positive instance of the skill).

Step 3: REVIEW AND RESTATE DEFINITION

"Complimenting means saying what you like about a person. What does complimenting mean?" SAYING WHAT YOU LIKE ABOUT A PERSON (Reinforce or correct)

Step 4: POSITIVE EXAMPLE

Video: One positive example (Debrief: Point out/discuss why the example is a positive instance of the skill).

Step 5: ACTIVITIES

Teacher models:

1a. "Listen to me compliment you." (Pay students various compliments, e.g., '(*student name*) I really like the way you are listening,' etc.).
b. "What are some other ways we can compliment people?" (Teacher leads discussion of various forms of compliments).

Students practice:

1. (Form a circle) "Now we are going to practice complimenting. I want everyone to think of a compliment you could give the person sitting next to you." (Teacher leads by paying the student next to him/her a compliment. Reinforce students' compliments or correct as needed).
2. "Pretend your class is having relays. The last person on your team just took the lead so your team won! What kind of compliment could you give your teammate?" (Give individual turns. Reinforce compliments which suggest the person did a great job or correct as needed).
3. "Let's say someone in your class just got off the swings so you could have a turn. How could you use complimenting to let that person know that was a nice thing to do?" (Give individual turns. Reinforce suggestions to compliment the person by saying IT WAS NICE, THANK YOU, etc., or correct).

Step 6: POSITIVE EXAMPLE

Video: Three positive examples (Debrief: Point out/discuss why the examples are positive instances of the skill).

Step 7: CRITERION ROLE PLAYS

1. "Let's pretend you're in gym class and the captains are choosing teams for a softball game. One of the captains chooses you. Tell me how you would compliment him for choosing you." (Give individual turns. *Criterion:* Students suggest: IT WAS NICE OF YOU TO CHOOSE ME, or THANK YOU FOR CHOOSING ME).
2. "Let's pretend you're having lunch and a boy at your table asks if you'd like one of his cookies. Tell me what you would say to let him know you like what he did." (Give individual turns. *Criterion:* Students suggest: THAT WAS NICE OF YOU, THANKS FOR SHARING, etc.).
3. "Let's pretend you're playing catch at recess, but one time when it's your turn to catch, the ball goes past you across the playground. A girl brings the ball back to you so you don't have to chase it. Tell me how you would compliment her." (*Criterion:* Students suggest: THANKS FOR GETTING THE BALL, or IT WAS NICE OF YOU TO GET THE BALL FOR ME, etc.).

Step 8: INFORMAL CONTRACTING

"Today in school I want you to compliment someone. What are you going to do today in school?" COMPLIMENT SOMEONE (Reinforce or correct)

VARIATIONS/ADAPTATIONS

GROUP	ACTIVITY	MATERIALS
Class or small group	• Review rule. Form a circle of students and tell them that we are going to say something nice about the person sitting next to us, e.g., teacher leads, compliments adjacent student.	None
Class or small group	• Review rule. Students write a paragraph about someone in their class, they write things they like about that person. Have students read their paragraph to class or group and then give their paragraph to the person they wrote about.	Pencil/paper
Class or small group	• Review rule. Have students list as many different compliments as they can think of. Pair off and act out times when they can be used.	Pencil/paper

AREA IV: Making Friends

SKILL #4: Friendship Making

NECESSARY PRESKILLS: Area II #1-9

REVIEW: Brief discussion of previous day's skill. Check to see if students followed informal contract.

Step 1: DEFINITION AND GUIDED DISCUSSION

Definition:

"Making friends means starting, taking turns talking, and inviting. What does making friends mean?"
STARTING, TAKING TURNS TALKING, AND INVITING (Reinforce or correct)
"Let's say this another way: Starting, taking turns talking, and inviting is called what?"
MAKING FRIENDS (Reinforce or correct)

Guided Discussion:

(Pair off students. Students should stay with same partner throughout guided discussion). "To make friends all you have to do is remember to put together some of the things you've already learned. First you have to remember *starting*. Starting means finding someone to talk to. What does starting mean?"
FINDING SOMEONE TO TALK TO (Reinforce or correct)
"A good way to start when you make friends is to trade names. What is a good way to start when you make friends?"
TRADE NAMES (Reinforce or correct)
"Watch me" (Teacher models with a student). "Hi, my name is ____, what's your name? Your turn to start by trading names." (Partners trade names. Reinforce trading names or correct).
"Next, you have to remember taking turns talking. Taking turns talking means you talk, then I talk, then you talk. What does taking turns talking mean?"
YOU TALK, THEN I TALK, THEN YOU TALK (Reinforce or correct)

"A good thing to take turns talking about when you make friends is things you both like to do. What is a good thing to take turns talking about when you make friends?"
THINGS YOU BOTH LIKE TO DO (Reinforce or correct)
"Watch me" (Teacher models with a student) "I like to play tag, what do you like to play?" (Continue conversation briefly). "Your turn to take turns talking about things you both like to do." (Partners take turns talking. Reinforce taking turns talking about things to do or correct). "The last thing you do to make friends is inviting. Inviting means asking someone to spend time with you. What does inviting mean?"
ASKING SOMEONE TO SPEND TIME WITH YOU (Reinforce or correct)
"A good way to invite when you make friends is to ask the person to play with you. What is a good way to invite when you make friends?"
ASK THE PERSON TO PLAY WITH YOU. (Reinforce or correct)
"Watch me." (Teacher models with a student) "(*student name*), would you like to play on the swings with me? Your turn to invite by asking the person to play with you." (Partners invite. Reinforce inviting or correct). "To make friends we use the rules for *starting* by trading names. Next, we use the rules for *taking turns talking* by taking turns talking about things we both like to do. Last, we use the rule for *inviting* by asking the person to play."

Step 2: POSITIVE EXAMPLE

Video: One positive example (Debrief: Point out/discuss why the example is a positive instance of the skill).

Step 3: REVIEW AND RESTATE DEFINITION

"Making friends means starting, taking turns talking, and inviting. What does making friends mean?"
STARTING, TAKING TURNS TALKING, AND INVITING (Reinforce or correct)

"First you can start by *trading names*. What do you do first?"
TRADE NAMES (Reinforce or correct)
"Next, you take turns talking about *things you both like to do*. What do you do next?"
TALK ABOUT THINGS YOU BOTH LIKE TO DO (Reinforce or correct)
"Last, you invite by *asking the person to play with you*. What do you do last?"
ASK THE PERSON TO PLAY (Reinforce or correct)

Step 4: POSITIVE EXAMPLE

Video: One positive example (Debrief: Point out/discuss why the example is a positive instance of the skill).

Step 5: ACTIVITIES

Teacher models:

1. (Select a student to model *starting* with) "Let's pretend we are on the playground. Let's say that I don't know you, but I want to make friends with you. *First*, I have to remember starting, *next*, taking turns talking, and *last*, inviting. Hi, my name is _____, what's your name?" (Student prompted to give name if needed) "That is starting. One thing I like to play is tether ball. What do you like to play?" (Student prompted to say at what he/she likes to play if needed. Continue conversation briefly). "That is taking turns talking. Would you like to play tether ball with me?" (Student prompted to respond if needed) "That is inviting."

Students practice:

1. (Pair off students) "We are going to practice making friends. I want you to pretend that you don't know your partner, but you want to make friends. First, I'll say *start* and I want you to trade names. Next, I'll say *take turns talking* and I want you to talk about things you like to do. Last, I'll say *invite* and I want you to ask your new friend to play with you. OK, let's get ready to make friends. Start." (Pause. Reinforce starting or

correct) "Take turns talking." (Pause. Reinforce taking turns talking or correct). "Invite." (Pause. Reinforce inviting or correct). (Have partners switch parts. Repeat activity).

2. (Pair off students) "This time let's pretend you and your partner are sitting in the cafeteria together. Let's say you don't know your partner, but you want to make friends. First, you have to remember starting, next, talking turns talking, and last, inviting. Show me how you would make friends." (Prompt interaction as needed. Have partners switch parts. Reinforce friendship making or correct).

3. (Pair off students) "Let's pretend you're on the playground after school. Your partner is playing there, too. You don't know your partner, but you want to make friends and play together. Show me how you would make friends. Remember to *start*, *take turns talking*, and *invite*." (Prompt interaction as needed. Have partners switch parts. Reinforce friendship making or correct).

Step 6: CRITERION ROLE PLAYS

1. (Pair off students) "Let's pretend that your school is going on a field trip and it's time for everyone to get on the school bus. You are the last person to get on the bus and there is only one seat left next to your partner. Let's say you don't know your partner, but you would like to make friends. Show me how you would use starting, taking turns talking, and inviting to make friends." (*Criterion:* Students initiate starting, taking turns talking, and inviting).

2. (Pair off students) "Let's pretend your partner is a new person in your class. It's time to go out to recess and your partner doesn't know any of the other kids at school yet. Show me how you would use starting, taking turns talking, and inviting to make friends with your partner." (*Criterion:* Students initiate starting, taking turns talking, and inviting).

3. (Pair off students) "Let's pretend it's recess time again. Two of your good friends you usually play with are absent from school today. You really want to play with someone. Pretend you see your partner bouncing a ball, but you don't know him/her. Show me how you would make friends with your partner so you can play together." (*Criterion:* Student initiates starting, taking turns talking, and inviting).

Step 7: INFORMAL CONTRACTING

"Next time you would like to make friends with someone, remember you can start by trading names, then taking turns talking about things you both like to do, and then, inviting the person to spend time with you. This week at recess I want you to try to make a new friend. What are you going to do this week?"

TRY TO MAKE A NEW FRIEND (Reinforce or correct)

VARIATIONS/ADAPTATIONS

GROUP	ACTIVITY	MATERIALS
Class or small group Individual	• Review rule. Read/tell students an incomplete story about two kids who are about to meet. Have students supply the ending by making up how they become friends.	Pre-planned story

VARIATIONS/ADAPTATIONS

GROUP	ACTIVITY	MATERIALS
Class or small group	• Review rule. Use transparency overlays to create a friendship making sequence. Start with a simple approach scene and add overlays showing the friends going through the steps. Ask students to tell you what is happening in their conversation by watching the progression of the overlays.	Transparencies
Class	• Review rule. Have students participate in a play. Students will act out parts of the play that will demonstrate how two people might meet and become friends.	Pre-planned student play

AREA IV REVIEW: Making Friends Skills

Step 1: RULE REVIEW AND PRACTICE

Rule Review:

"Good grooming means being neat and clean. Being neat and clean is called what?"
GOOD GROOMING (Reinforce or correct)

Practice:

"What are some things you should do to be neat and clean?"
WASH HANDS AND FACE, BRUSH TEETH, WEAR CLEAN CLOTHES, etc. (Reinforce or correct)

Rule Review:

"Smiling shows you like someone or are having fun. How do you show you like someone or that you're having fun?"
SMILE (Reinforce or correct)

Practice:

"Let's *do it*. Pretend we are all playing catch together and having a good time!"
Students SMILE (Reinforce or correct)

Rule Review:

"Saying what you like about a person is complimenting. Saying what you like about a person is called what?"
COMPLIMENTING (Reinforce or correct)

Practice:

"Give me" (or another student in group) "a compliment"
Students COMPLIMENT (Reinforce or correct)

Rule Review:

"Making friends means starting, taking turns talking, and inviting. What do you do when you make friends?"

START, TAKE TURNS TALKING, AND INVITE (Reinforce or correct)

Practice:

"Pretend you don't know me." (or another student in group) "Show me how you would make friends. First, *start* by trading names, then *take turns talking* about things you both like to do, then *invite* the person to spend time with you."
Students practice *starting, taking turns talking,* and *inviting*. (Reinforce trading names, taking turns talking, and inviting, or go through correction procedure).

Step 2: ROLE PLAY

1. "Here's a chance to use all the Making Friends Skills. First, let's talk about good grooming."
(If student is neat and clean, give specific praise. If grooming could be improved, give specific suggestions). "Next, let's pretend I'm sitting next to you on a bus going on a field trip and you'd like to make friends with me. While we're taking turns talking, I'd also like you to show me you're having a good time and to give me a compliment" (Repeat role play individually with each student in group). (Reinforce *Making Friends, Smiling,* and *Complimenting*, or reteach skill).

AREA V: Coping Skills

SKILL #1: When Someone Says "No"

NECESSARY PRESKILLS: Area II #1–9

REVIEW: Brief discussion of previous day's skill. Check to see if students followed informal contract.

Step 1: DEFINITION AND GUIDED DISCUSSION

Definition:

"When someone says 'no' you should find another way to play. What should you do when someone says 'no'?"
FIND ANOTHER WAY TO PLAY (Reinforce or correct)
"When should you find another way to play?"
WHEN SOMEONE SAYS "NO" (Reinforce or correct)
"Cindy asked Sarah if she could play hopscotch with her. Sarah said 'no!' What should Cindy do when someone says 'no'?"
FIND ANOTHER WAY TO PLAY (Reinforce or correct)
"Bobby asked Pam if he could play marbles with her. Pam said 'no'. What should Bobby do when someone says 'no'?"
FIND ANOTHER WAY TO PLAY (Reinforce or correct)
"When should you find another way to play?"
WHEN SOMEONE SAYS "NO" (Reinforce or correct)

Guided Discussion:

"Sometimes when you ask people if you can play with them, they say 'no'. Has that ever happened to you?" (Discuss) "When someone says 'no' to you, you have to figure out another way to play. There are lots of things you can do to find another way to play. One way is to ask if you can take turns by waiting until someone is out. What's one way to find another way to play?"
ASK IF YOU CAN TAKE TURNS (Reinforce or correct)
"Another way is to make the game bigger by getting another toy. What's another way?"
MAKE THE GAME BIGGER (Reinforce or correct)
"Sometimes people say 'no' because they just don't want you to play with them at all. When this

happens, you should go play with someone else. What should you do if someone doesn't want to play with you at all?"
PLAY WITH SOMEONE ELSE (Reinforce or correct)

Step 2: POSITIVE EXAMPLE

Video: One positive example (Debrief: Point out/discuss why the example is a positive instance of the skill).

Step 3: NEGATIVE EXAMPLE

Video: One negative example (Debrief: Point out/discuss why the example is *not* a positive instance of the skill).

Step 4: REVIEW AND RESTATE DEFINITION

"When someone says 'no', you should find another way to play. What should you do when someone says 'no'?"
FIND ANOTHER WAY TO PLAY (Reinforce or correct)

Step 5: POSITIVE EXAMPLE

Video: One positive example (Debrief: Point out/discuss why the example is a positive instance of the skill).

Step 6: ACTIVITIES

A. Teacher models:

1. "Remember, if someone tells you 'no', there are other things you can do to find another way to play. One thing you might do is ask if you can *take turns* playing. Let's say some people are jumping rope. I ask if I can join them and they say, 'no, we're using the rope'. I might ask them if they will take turns with me."

Students practice:

1. "Let's say some kids are playing four-square and you want to play, too. You ask if you can join them and they tell you, 'no, we have four people playing'. What could you do?" (Reinforce suggestions to ask to take turns, or correct).
2. "Let's say you want to play on the swings at recess, but all the swings are taken. What could you do?" (Reinforce suggestions to take turns, or correct).
3. "Pretend a boy in your class brought his new bike to school. You ask if you can ride it, but he says he already promised it to someone else. What could you ask him?"(Reinforce suggestions to ask to take turns, or correct).

B. Teacher models:

1. "Another thing you can do to find another way to play is to make the game bigger. Let's say some kids are playing with modeling clay. I ask if I can play with them, too and they tell me, 'No, we really don't have enough clay'. I might go see if I can find more clay so that I can play, too."

Students practice:

1. "Let's say you see some kids who are building a tower with blocks. You ask if you can build the tower with them and they say, 'no, we don't have enough blocks'. You look around and see more blocks across the room. What could you do?" (Reinforce suggestions to get more blocks, or correct).
2. "Pretend some students in your class are drawing on the chalkboard. You would like to draw, too, but they tell you there isn't enough chalk. What could you do?"
GET MORE CHALK (Reinforce or correct)

C. Teacher models:

1. "Sometimes you have to find another way to play by playing something else or playing with other people. Let's say some kids are playing tag. I ask them if I can join the game and they tell me, 'no, we don't want to play with you, we want to

play alone'. If this happens I would say, 'OK. I'll go play with someone else.'"

Students practice:

1. "Let's pretend some kids are having fun playing on the bars. You ask if you can play with them and they tell you, 'No, we don't want to play with you, we want to play by ourselves'. What should you do?" (Reinforce suggestions to play something else, or correct).
2. "Let's pretend two kids are bouncing a ball back and forth. You ask if you can play, too and they say, 'No, we don't want to play with you'. What should you do?" (Reinforce suggestions to go play something else, or correct).
3. "Pretend your class is going to the library. You ask some students if you can sit with them and they say, 'No, we're going to work on a project together'. What should you do?" (Reinforce suggestions to sit with someone else).

Step 7: POSITIVE EXAMPLE

Video: Two positive examples (Debrief: Point out/discuss why the examples are positive instances of the skill).

Step 8: CRITERION ROLE PLAY

1. "Let's pretend two people in your class are using cups of water to water the plants in your classroom. You ask them if you can water the plants with them and they say, 'No, we only have two cups'. Tell me what you would do." (*Criterion:* Students suggest either asking to take turns or going to get another cup of water).
2. "Let's pretend you're out on the playground and you see two people you know talking together on the field. You ask if you can join them and they say, 'No, we want to be alone'. Tell me what you would do." (*Criterion:* Students suggest they should go play with someone else or do something else).
3. "Let's pretend two students are playing catch on the playground. You would like to play, too, but they say they don't want to play three-way catch. Tell me what you would do." (*Criterion:* Students suggest either getting another ball and someone else to play with, or choosing to play something else).

Step 9: INFORMAL CONTRACTING

"Next time you ask to play with someone and they say 'no', remember what we talked about and find another way to play. There are lots of ways to find another way to play. You choose the best way. Remember, when someone says 'no', you are going to find another way to play. What are you going to do when someone says 'no'?"
FIND ANOTHER WAY TO PLAY (Reinforce or correct)

VARIATIONS/ADAPTATIONS

GROUP	ACTIVITY	MATERIALS
Small group, large group or class	• Review rule. Tell student(s) they are going to play blocks. The rule is they cannot put one on top of another. They have to find another way to play with the blocks.	Blocks
Small group, large group or class	• Review rule. Student(s) have sharing/show and tell. The rule is they cannot talk. They have to find another way to show and tell.	None

AREA V: Coping Skills

SKILL #2: When You Express Anger

NECESSARY PRESKILLS: Area II #1-9

REVIEW: Brief discussion of previous day's skill. Check to see if students followed informal contract.

Step 1: DEFINITION AND GUIDED DISCUSSION

Definition:

"When you express anger you should say why you are mad without hurting. When you express anger you should do what?"
SAY WHY YOU'RE (I'M) MAD WITHOUT HURTING (Reinforce or correct)
"Let's say this another way. When you say you are mad without hurting, you are *expressing anger the right way*. When you say why you are mad without hurting, you are doing what?"
EXPRESSING ANGER THE RIGHT WAY (Reinforce or correct)
"Linda told Ronnie why she was mad without hurting him. Linda was doing what?"
EXPRESSING ANGER THE RIGHT WAY (Reinforce or correct)
"How do we know Linda was expressing anger the right way?"
SHE/LINDA SAID WHY SHE WAS MAD WITHOUT HURTING
"When you tell someone why you are mad without hurting, you are expressing anger the right way. When you tell someone why you are mad without hurting, you are doing what?"
EXPRESSING ANGER THE RIGHT WAY (Reinforce or correct)

Guided Discussion:

"When you are angry you have the feeling that you are unhappy with someone. When you tell someone *why* you are mad at him or her you are showing your anger the right way. What's the right way to show your anger?"
TELL WHY YOU'RE (I'M) ANGRY/MAD (Reinforce or correct)
"When you tell someone why you are angry you are letting the person know you are mad without hurting him/her. Does it make you mad when someone wrecks something you're working on?"
YES (If NO ask "What makes you angry?" or suggest, "Does it make you mad when someone does something mean, like tripping you or throwing something at you? If that happens you need to tell the person you're mad without hurting him/her").

Step 2: POSITIVE EXAMPLE

Video: One positive example (Debrief: Point out/discuss why the example is a positive instance of the skill).

Step 3: NEGATIVE EXAMPLE

Video: One negative example (Debrief: Point out/discuss why the example is *not* a positive instance of the skill).

Step 4: REVIEW AND RESTATE DEFINITION

"When you express anger you should say why you are mad without hurting. When you express anger you should do what?"
SAY WHY YOU'RE (I'M) MAD WITHOUT HURTING (Reinforce or correct)

Step 5: POSITIVE EXAMPLE

Video: One positive example (Debrief: Point out/discuss why the example is a positive instance of the skill).

Step 6: ACTIVITIES

Teacher models:

1. "Watch me show you how to express anger the

right way. It's lunch time. When I'm not looking, someone takes my cookies. I might say, 'That wasn't nice of you. That really makes me mad. Please give my cookies back.' I showed that I was mad without hurting someone."

Students practice:

1. "Let's practice getting angry in the right way. I'll be a student who walks by your desk and takes something without asking you. Show me what you would do." (Give individual turns. Reinforce expressing anger appropriately, or correct).
2. (Pair off students) "Let's try another one. Let's say you and your partner are playing together and I keep butting in and ruining your game. Show me how you would express your anger." (Reinforce expressing anger appropriately, or correct).
3. "Let's pretend you build a model airplane and brought it to school to show the class. A boy in your class took it without asking and broke part of it. Show me how you would express your anger." (Reinforce or correct)

Step 7: POSITIVE EXAMPLE

Video: Two positive examples (Debrief: Point out/discuss why the examples are positive instances of the skill).

Step 8: CRITERION ROLE PLAYS

1. "You are playing a game of tag at recess. You tag another student and tell him he's 'it'. He says you didn't tag him and it makes you mad that he didn't follow the rules. Show me how you would express your anger without hurting." (*Criterion:* Answers that show the student is mad without hurting).
2. (Pair off students) "Pretend your partner is a student in your class who takes your bike and rides it without asking you first. It makes you angry that your partner took it without asking you. Show me how you would express your anger the right way." (*Criterion:* Answers that show student is angry without hurting).
3. "Pretend you are walking to your desk and a student puts out his foot and trips you so you almost fall down. You think it was a mean thing to do and it makes you angry. Show me how you would express your anger the right way." (*Criterion:* Answers that show student is angry without hurting).

Step 9: INFORMAL CONTRACTING

"Next time someone makes you mad you need to say why you are mad without hurting the person. Next time someone makes you mad, what are you going to do?"
SAY WHY YOU ARE MAD (I AM MAD) WITHOUT HURTING (Reinforce or correct)

VARIATIONS/ADAPTATIONS

GROUP	ACTIVITY	MATERIALS
Small group, large group or class	• Review rule. Student(s) come up with a list of things that make them angry. Then the student(s) discuss how you could tell someone you're mad without hurting them.	None

AREA V: Coping Skills

SKILL #3: When Someone Teases

NECESSARY PRESKILLS: Area II #1-9

REVIEW: Brief discussion of previous day's skill. Check to see if students followed informal contract.

Step 1: DEFINITION AND GUIDED DISCUSSION

Definition:

"When someone teases you, you should look away and not answer. When someone teases you, you should do what?"
LOOK AWAY AND NOT ANSWER (Reinforce or correct)
"When should you look away and not answer?"
WHEN SOMEONE TEASES YOU (Reinforce or correct)
"Kevin is teasing Gail. What should Gail do?"
LOOK AWAY AND NOT ANSWER (Reinforce or correct)
"Susan is teasing Stephanie. What should Stephanie do?"
LOOK AWAY AND NOT ANSWER (Reinforce or correct)
"When should you look away and not answer?"
WHEN SOMEONE TEASES YOU (Reinforce or correct)

Guided Discussion:

"Teasing is when someone says something or does something to bother you. When this happens to you, look away and don't answer. When the people who are teasing see that you aren't bothered by it, they will usually stop. When someone pokes you, this can be teasing. If you don't like it, walk away and don't say anything. When someone calls you a silly name, this can be teasing. What should you do?"
LOOK AWAY AND DON'T ANSWER (Reinforce or correct)

Step 2: POSITIVE EXAMPLE

Video: One positive example (Debrief: Point out/discuss why the example is a positive instance of the skill).

Step 3: NEGATIVE EXAMPLE

Video: One negative example (Debrief: Point out/discuss why the example is *not* a positive instance of the skill).

Step 4: REVIEW AND RESTATE DEFINITION

"When someone teases you, you should look away and not answer. What should you do when someone teases you?"
LOOK AWAY AND NOT ANSWER (Reinforce or correct)

Step 5: POSITIVE EXAMPLE

Video: One positive example (Debrief: Point out/discuss why the example is a positive instance of the skill).

Step 6: ACTIVITIES

Teacher models:

1. "Watch me show you what to do when someone teases you. Let's pretend someone just called me 'stupid'. I look away and don't answer, like this." (Teacher looks away).

Students practice:

1. "Let's pretend you're at recess. Someone runs by you and calls you a 'bozo'. Show me what you should do when someone teases you like that." (Reinforce looking away and not answering, or correct).
2. "Show me what you would do if someone teases you by saying you have ants in your pants." (Reinforce looking away and not answering, or correct).

3. "Show me what you would do if someone tried to tease you by poking at you." (Teacher pokes at students repeatedly). (Reinforce looking away and not answering, or correct).

Step 7: POSITIVE EXAMPLE

Video: Three positive examples (Debrief: Point out/discuss why the examples are positive instances of the skill).

Step 8: CRITERION ROLE PLAYS

1. "In your reading group a classmate teases you about missing a word. Show me what you should do." (*Criterion:* Students look away and don't answer).
2. "You're on the playground playing jumprope with some other students. It's your turn to jump and you miss a jump right away. One of the other children laughs at you. Show me what you should do." (*Criterion:* Students look away and don't answer).
3. "You're talking to your best friend at recess and a boy from another grade comes up and calls you a 'weirdo' in front of your friend. Show me what you should do." (*Criterion:* Students look away and don't answer).

Step 9: INFORMAL CONTRACTING

"The next time someone teases you I want you to look away and not answer. What are you going to do the next time someone teases you?"
LOOK AWAY AND NOT ANSWER (Reinforce or correct)

VARIATIONS/ADAPTATIONS

GROUP	ACTIVITY	MATERIALS
Small group, large group or class	• Review rule. Each child gets to tell about a situation in which they were teased. At the end they would tell the right way to deal with the teasing (look away and don't answer).	None
Small group, large group or class	• Review rule. Two students are given puppets. One person's puppet teases the other person's puppet. The person being teased has to show the right way to deal with the teasing (look away and don't answer).	Puppets

AREA V: Coping Skills

SKILL #4: When Someone Tries to Hurt You

NECESSARY PRESKILLS: Area II #1-9

(*Please note:* The components of this skill may misrepresent established school rules or be unacceptable to some teachers and/or parents. Use discretion).

REVIEW: Brief discussion of previous day's skill. Check to see if students followed informal contract.

Step 1: DEFINITION AND GUIDED DISCUSSION

Definition:

"When someone tries to hurt you, you should try to walk away. Don't fight back unless you have to. When someone tries to hurt you, what should you do?"
TRY TO WALK AWAY. DON'T FIGHT BACK UNLESS YOU (I) HAVE TO (Reinforce or correct)
"When should you try to walk away?"
WHEN SOMEONE TRIES TO HURT YOU (ME) (Reinforce or correct)
"When should you *not* fight back unless you have to?"
WHEN SOMEONE TRIES TO HURT YOU (ME) (Reinforce or correct)
"Dan is trying to hurt Larry. What should Larry do?"
TRY TO WALK AWAY/NOT FIGHT BACK UNLESS HE HAS TO (Reinforce or correct)
"When someone tries to hurt you, what should you *not* do unless you have to?"
FIGHT BACK (Reinforce or correct)
"When someone tries to hurt you, what should you try to do?"
WALK AWAY (Reinforce or correct)

Guided Discussion:

"Sometimes people get mad at each other. Sometimes they get so mad they try to get into a fight. If someone gets mad and tries to hurt you, the best thing to do is just walk away. What should you do if someone tries to hurt you?"
WALK AWAY (Reinforce or correct)
"If someone grabs you and you can't get away, yell for help. What should you do if someone grabs you and tries to get you into a fight?"
YELL FOR HELP (Reinforce or correct)
"If no one is nearby to help you, you might have to push the person away and then get away from him/her. What should you do if no one is nearby?"
PUSH THE PERSON AWAY (Reinforce or correct)
"Most of the time this *won't* happen, but you should try to get away from the person as soon as you can. Remember, when someone gets mad at you and you think they might try to hurt you, the best thing to do is walk away."

Step 2: POSITIVE EXAMPLE

Video: One positive example (Debrief: Point out/discuss why the example is a positive instance of the skill).

Step 3: REVIEW AND RESTATE DEFINITION

"When someone tries to hurt you, you should try to walk away. Don't fight back unless you have to. What should you do when someone tries to hurt you?"
WALK AWAY. DON'T FIGHT BACK UNLESS YOU (I) HAVE TO (Reinforce or correct)

Step 4: ACTIVITIES

A. Teacher models:

1. "Let's pretend someone is trying to hurt me and make me fight. The *first* thing I would do is try to walk away like this." (Teacher walks away).

Students practice:

1. "If someone is trying to hurt you, show me the first thing you should try to do." (Reinforce students for walking away, or correct).
2. "Pretend someone on the playground said you cheated in a game and tried to get you to fight. Show me what you should do when the person starts trying to hurt you." (Reinforce students for walking away, or correct).
3. "Pretend you and a friend are playing and you start wrestling. At first it's fun, but then your friends gets mad and really starts trying to hurt you. Show me what you should do." (Reinforce students for walking away, or correct).

B. Teacher models:

1. "Let's say a student tries to hurt me by grabbing me. I can't seem to get away from him, but other people are nearby. I should call for help like this: 'Help me! He's hurting me!'"

Students practice:

1. "Let's say someone tried to hurt you by grabbing you. You can't get away, but other people are nearby. Show me what you should do." (Reinforce calling for help, or correct)
2. Pretend a student walks up to you and grabs you around the neck. You can't get away, but you see a teacher nearby. Show me what you should do." (Reinforce students for calling for help, or correct).

C. Teacher models:

1. "This won't happen very often, but let's say someone is trying to hurt me and I *can't* get away. Nobody is nearby to help me. If this happens, I might have to push the person away *first*, and *then* get away." (Role play pushing an imaginary person away and walking away).

Students practice:

1. "Your turn again. Let's say someone is trying to hurt you and you *cannot* get away. Nobody is close by to help you. There are two things you might have to do. What are they?"
PUSH THE PERSON AWAY, THEN GET AWAY (Reinforce or correct)
"Do it" (Reinforce students pushing away imaginary person and getting away, or correct).
2. "Pretend someone jumps on you when you are out on the field at recess. You can't see who it is, but the person is trying to hurt you. Nobody is on the field to help you. Show me what you should do." (Reinforce students pushing away imaginary person and getting away, or correct).
3. "Pretend someone walks up to you on the playground and says you called them a creep. You see that this person is really mad and you know you did not call them a creep. Pretend this person starts to try to hurt you. What is the *first* thing you should try to do?"
WALK AWAY (Reinforce or correct)
"Do it. But, let's say you can't walk away. You see a teacher on duty. What should you do *next*?" (Reinforce responses which include calling for help, or correct).
"Do it. What if you couldn't get away and there was no teacher around to help you. What should you do then?" (Reinforce responses which include pushing the person away and then getting away).
"Do it."

Step 5: POSITIVE EXAMPLE

Video: Three positive examples (Debrief: Point out/discuss why the examples are positive instances of the skill).

Step 6: CRITERION ROLE PLAYS

1. "Let's pretend you are bouncing a ball on the playground by yourself. Someone your size runs up to you and tries to start a fight with you. Show me the first thing you should try to do." (*Criterion:* Students walk away).
2. "Let's pretend you and a friend are swinging

on the swings. Someone tries to push you out. A lot of other people are nearby. Show me what you should do." (*Criterion:* Students call for help).

3. "Let's pretend you are in the park and you have walked off by yourself. A kid grabs you and no one is around to help. Show me what two things you should do." (*Criterion:* Student pushes imaginary person and then walks away).

Step 7: INFORMAL CONTRACTING

"Remember, if someone tries to hurt you, you should try to walk away. Don't fight back unless you really have to. If someone tries to hurt you, what are you going to do?"
WALK AWAY. DON'T FIGHT BACK UNLESS YOU (I) HAVE TO (Reinforce or correct)

VARIATIONS/ADAPTATIONS

GROUP	ACTIVITY	MATERIALS
Small group, large group or class	• Review rule. Student(s) come up with a list of times when someone might try to hurt them. Then the student(s) discuss how they would deal with the situations.	None

AREA V: Coping Skills

SKILL #5: When Someone Asks You To Do Something You Can't Do

NECESSARY PRESKILLS: Area II #1-9

REVIEW: Brief discussion of previous day's skill. Check to see if students followed informal contract.

Step 1: DEFINITION AND GUIDED DISCUSSION

Definition:

"When someone asks you to do something you can't do, you should say 'no' politely. When someone asks you to do something you can't do, what should you do?"
SAY "NO" POLITELY (Reinforce or correct)
"When should you say 'no' politely?"
WHEN SOMEONE ASKS YOU (ME) TO DO SOMETHING YOU (I) CAN'T DO (Reinforce or correct)
"Let's try these: Carolyn's friend asks her to play. Carolyn can't play right now. What should Carolyn do?"
SAY "NO" POLITELY (Reinforce or correct)
"Don's brother asks him to help him. Don can't help right now. What should Don do?"
SAY "NO" POLITELY (Reinforce or correct)
"When someone asks you to do something you can't do, you should say 'no' politely. When should you say 'no' politely?"
WHEN SOMEONE ASKS YOU (ME) TO DO SOMETHING YOU (I) CAN'T DO (Reinforce or correct)

Guided Discussion:

"Sometimes you have to say 'no' when friends ask you to help them, share something with them, or do them a favor. Maybe you can't help them because you are too busy, or don't want to share something. When you say 'no', you need to say it in a polite way. You need to say why you can't do

it. What's a polite thing to do when you have to say 'no' to someone?"
TELL WHY YOU CAN'T DO IT (Reinforce or correct)

"That way you won't make people mad or hurt their feelings. If someone asked you to come play records, but you were busy reading, you might say this: 'No thank you, I'm reading right now.' That way you would be saying 'no' politely and telling why you couldn't play."

Step 2: POSITIVE EXAMPLE

Video: One positive example (Debrief: Point out/discuss why the example is a positive instance of the skill).

Step 3: NEGATIVE EXAMPLE

Video: One negative example (Debrief: Point out/discuss why the example is *not* a positive instance of the skill).

Step 4: REVIEW AND RESTATE DEFINITION

"When someone asks you to do something you can't do, you should say 'no' politely. What should you do when someone asks you to do something you can't do?"
SAY "NO" POLITELY (Reinforce or correct)

Step 5: POSITIVE EXAMPLE

Video: One positive example (Debrief: Point out/discuss why the example is a positive instance of the skill).

Step 6: ACTIVITIES

Teacher Models:

1. "If you asked me to sit by you at lunch, but I can't because I already told other friends I'd sit by them, I'd say, 'No, I can't sit by you this time because I'm already sitting with some other people.' That way I'm saying 'no' politely."
2. "If you asked me to play on the bars at recess, but I wanted to play jumprope, I might say, 'No thanks, I want to play jumprope today.' That would be saying 'no' a polite way."

Students practice:

1. "Let's pretend you are working on some math problems and there are only five minutes left to finish. You're very busy working and I ask you to help me collect the lunch tickets. Tell me how you would tell me 'no' politely." (Give individual turns. Reinforce a polite 'no', or correct).
2. "Let's try another one. Let's pretend you are having free time and you've been waiting to play checkers. I ask you if you want to play cards with me, but you don't want to play cards right now. Tell me how you would say 'no' to me politely." (Give individual turns. Reinforce a polite 'no', or correct).
3. "You're playing with some friends at recess and another friend asks you to play a different game. You're having fun and don't want to stop playing with your friends. Tell me how you would say 'no' politely." (Give individual turns. Reinforce a polite 'no', or correct).

Step 7: POSITIVE EXAMPLE

Video: Three positive examples (Debrief: Point out/discuss why the examples are positive instances of the skill).

Step 8: CRITERION ROLE PLAYS

1. "Let's pretend you saved your money and just bought a new ball. I ask you if I can use it, but you're having fun playing with it and don't want to let me use it. Tell me how you would say 'no' to me in a polite way." (Give individual turns. *Criterion:* Polite "no").
2. "Let's pretend that after lunch you start feeling a little sick, so when a friend asks you to play with him at recess, you really don't want to. Tell

me how you would say 'no' without hurting his feelings." (Give individual turns. *Criterion:* Polite "no").

3. "Let's pretend a girl in your class asked you to sit with her on the bus after school. You already planned to walk over to another friend's house to play after school. Tell me how you would say 'no' politely to the girl." (Give individual turns. *Criterion:* Polite "no").

Step 9: INFORMAL CONTRACTING

"Remember, it's OK to say 'no' politely when someone asks you to do something you can't do. Next time someone asks you to do something you can't do, say 'no' politely. What are you going to do next time someone asks you to do something you can't do?"
SAY "NO" POLITELY (Reinforce or correct)

VARIATIONS/ADAPTATIONS

GROUP	ACTIVITY	MATERIALS
Small group, large group or class	• Review rule. Student(s) come up with a list of things they can't do. Then the students discuss how they would deal with the situation if they were asked to do something they can't do.	None

AREA V: Coping Skills

SKILL #6: When Things Don't Go Right

NECESSARY PRESKILLS: Area II #1-9

REVIEW: Brief discussion of previous day's skill. Check to see if students followed informal contract.

Step 1: DEFINITION AND GUIDED DISCUSSION

Definition:

"When things don't go right you should try another way. When things don't go right what should you do?"
TRY ANOTHER WAY (Reinforce or correct)
"When should you try another way?"
WHEN THINGS DON'T GO RIGHT (Reinforce or correct)

"Let's try these: Marie is trying to make a paper airplane and things aren't going right. What should Marie do?"
TRY ANOTHER WAY (Reinforce or correct)
"Amy and Jack want to listen to records and things aren't going right. What should Amy and Jack do?"
TRY ANOTHER WAY (Reinforce or correct)
"When should you try another way?"
WHEN THINGS DON'T GO RIGHT (Reinforce or correct)

Guided Discussion:

"Sometimes, no matter what you do nothing will go right. When things don't go right you have to try another way. If someone you want to play with ignores you, what should you do?"
FIND SOMEONE ELSE (Reinforce or correct)
"If you try to do something and find it's too hard, you could ask a friend or teacher for help. When things don't go right what should you do?"
TRY ANOTHER WAY (Reinforce or correct)

Step 2: POSITIVE EXAMPLE

(Teacher models positive example) "Let's pretend I've been thinking all day about playing on the bars at recess. I run over to the bars and they're full. I would try another way by playing something else." (Debrief: Point out/discuss why the example is a positive instance of the skill).

Step 3: NEGATIVE EXAMPLE

(Teacher models negative example) "Tom is having a hard time doing his math worksheet, so he begins to cry." (Debrief: Point out/discuss why the example is *not* a positive instance of the skill).

Step 4: REVIEW AND RESTATE DEFINITION

"When things don't go right, try another way. What should you do when things don't go right?" TRY ANOTHER WAY (Reinforce or correct)

Step 5: POSITIVE EXAMPLE

(Teacher models positive example) "Let's pretend I was very careful that my worksheet was super neat. Just as I was about to hand it in to my teacher, the student next to me spilled paint on it. I would try another way by telling the teacher and then doing it over." (Debrief: Point out/discuss why the example is a positive instance of the skill).

Step 6: ACTIVITIES

Teacher models:

1. "Watch and listen to me while I *try another way*. Let's pretend I want to go outside and play, but it's raining and I have to stay inside. What can I do instead? I know! I can ask one of my friends to play checkers with me. My friend and I go to play checkers, but all of the games are being used. What can we do now? Well, we can wait for one of the games to be free, or we can play another game, or maybe we can read books. I could talk to my friend and decide. My friend and I decide to read books. Instead of giving up, we still had fun by trying something else."

Students practice:

1. "All right, it's your turn to try *finding another way*. Let's pretend you go out to the playground and see one of your friends sitting by him/herself. You want to play with this friend, but your friend just wants to sit alone. Tell me how you might try another way." (Give individual turns. Reinforce various suggestions to do something else, or correct).
2. "Let's say you bought a new model airplane. You were sure you could put it together, but once you started, it was harder than you thought. Tell me some things you could do to try another way." (Give individual turns. Reinforce various suggestions to get help, do something else, or correct).
3. "Let's pretend you invited a friend to your house to watch a special television show after school. When you turn the t.v. on you find out it's broken and you can't watch the program. Tell me how you might try another way." (Give individual turns. Reinforce various suggestions to do something else, or correct).

Step 7: CRITERION ROLE PLAYS

1. "Let's pretend you have free play. You choose a puzzle that turns out to be too hard. Show me what you would do to try another way." (Give individual turns. *Criterion:* Students suggest getting help or various other free time activities they might do instead).
2. "Let's pretend you don't have any pencils to do your homework. You go to the school store and they are out of pencils. Show me what you could do to try another way." (Give individual turns. *Criterion:* Students suggest asking another student for a pencil, borrowing one from the teacher, etc.).

3. "Let's pretend you saw a t.v. show you loved. You couldn't wait to share it during Show and Tell, but the student before you got up and told all about the same show. Show how you could try another way." (*Criterion:* Students suggest talking about something else for Show and Tell).

Step 8: INFORMAL CONTRACTING

"Next time things don't go right I want you to try another way. What are you going to do when things don't go right?"
TRY ANOTHER WAY (Reinforce or correct)

VARIATIONS/ADAPTATIONS

GROUP	ACTIVITY	MATERIALS
Small group, large group or class	• Review rule. Each student tells a situation when things didn't go right. Discuss what you could do (try another way) in these situations.	None

AREA V REVIEW: Coping Skills

Step 1: RULE REVIEW AND PRACTICE

Rule Review:

"When someone says 'no' you should find another way to play. What should you do when someone says 'no'?"
FIND ANOTHER WAY TO PLAY (Reinforce or correct)

Practice:

"Pretend you asked a friend to play with you, but he said, 'No, not right now', what would you do?"
ASK SOMEONE ELSE TO PLAY/FIND SOMETHING ELSE TO DO (Reinforce or correct)

Rule Review:

"To express anger the right way you should say why you're mad without hurting. What should you do to express anger the right way?"
SAY WHY YOU'RE MAD WITHOUT HURTING (Reinforce or correct)

Practice:

"Pretend someone took a cookie from your lunch tray when you weren't looking. Show me what you would do."
(Reinforce expressing anger verbally, or correct)

Rule Review:

"When someone teases you, you should look away and don't answer. What should you do when someone teases you?"
LOOK AWAY. DON'T ANSWER (Reinforce or correct)

Practice:

"Let's pretend someone called you a name. Show me what you would do."
(Reinforce ignoring teasing, or correct)

Rule Review:

"When someone tries to hurt you, you should walk

away. Don't fight back unless you have to. What should you do if someone tries to hurt you?"
WALK AWAY. DON'T FIGHT BACK UNLESS YOU HAVE TO (Reinforce or correct)

Practice:

"Let's say someone gets very mad at you during recess and tries to get into a fight. Show me what you would do. Pretend the person grabs you and you can't get away. You see a teacher on playground duty. Show me what you would do. What if there was no one around to help you? Show me what you would do then."
(Reinforce walking away, calling for help, and shoving the person away and getting away, or correct).

Rule Review

"When someone asks you to do something you can't do you should say 'no' politely. What should you do when someone asks you to do something you can't do?"
SAY "NO" POLITELY (Reinforce or correct)

Practice:

"Let's say a friend asks you to play with him at recess, but you're already planning to play with other friends. What would you do?"
(Reinforce polite "no", or correct)

Rule Review:

"When things don't go right you should try another way. What should you do when things don't go right?"
TRY ANOTHER WAY (Reinforce or correct)

Practice:

"Let's say you were looking forward to recess, but it starts raining and you can't go out. What would you do? The first person you ask to play with you says, 'No, I just want to read during recess.' What would you do then?"
(Reinforce finding someone/something else to play with inside, and reinforce asking someone else to play with, or correct)

Step 2: ROLE PLAY

1. "Now use *all* of the coping skills. Pretend you really want to play softball during lunch recess. On your way out to the field a friend asks you to play four-square. Show me what you would do."
(Reinforce *saying no politely*, or reteach skill).
2. "When you get to the diamond, they're choosing teams. You ask if you can play first base, but the team captain says somebody is already playing on first. Show me what you would do."
(Reinforce suggesting another position or reteach *when someone says "no"*).
3. "You're playing in right field and someone hits a fly ball. You think you've got it, but you drop it. A couple of kids start calling you butterfingers. Show me what you would do."
(Reinforce ignoring, or reteach *when someone teases you*).
4. "You're at bat and someone on the other team says you've got three strikes when you know you've only got two. You're getting kind of mad about it. Show me what you would do."
(Reinforce expressing anger verbally, or reteach *expressing anger*).
5. "You get a hit, but the first baseman says he tagged you and you should be out. You know you're safe, so you stay there. He starts shoving you and trying to get you to fight. What do you do?"
(Reinforce walking away, getting help, or reteach *when someone tries to hurt you*).
6. "You play for a little longer, but everybody starts arguing and it's really not much fun. What would you do?"
(Reinforce finding another activity, or reteach *when things don't go right*).

Section VI: Behavior Management Procedures

As noted in Section IV, the ACCEPTS program contains a behavior management component that encourages the use of previously taught social skills within natural settings such as the classroom and playground. A question that frequently arises is whether formal behavior management procedures are necessary to achieve this goal.

It is possible that the teaching and instructional mastery of classroom behavioral competencies would improve the level of appropriate classroom behavior and similarly, that the teaching/mastery of peer-to-peer social skills would improve social competence and peer acceptance. The evidence is not completely clear on this question at present. However, this is an effect that should not be counted on to occur naturally or automatically — especially with handicapped children.

Unless special reasons exist for not doing so, the authors recommend that classroom and peer-to-peer social skills be taught using the guidelines described in Section IV and then behavior management procedures implemented in classroom and playground settings to support/strengthen their use. This section describes guidelines, procedures, and forms for implementing both classroom and playground behavior management procedures that have been extensively tested by the authors.

An individual contingency system with individual backup rewards and a response cost component is used to *increase* appropriate and to *decrease* inappropriate classroom behavior. A combined individual-group contingency with shared activity rewards and peer involvement is used to strengthen peer-to-peer social skills during playground interactions. These two systems are based upon the following assumptions:

(1) The ACCEPTS instructional and behavior management procedures will effectively teach classroom and peer-to-peer social skills to the broad range of mildly and moderately handicapped children. Special adaptations of both would be required for use with severely handicapped children.
(2) In most cases, it is necessary to implement a contingency management system in classroom and playground setting to ensure that (a) the skills taught will be used, and (b) that an actual impact on classroom and playground behavior will be achieved.
(3) The management system should be as simple, unobtrusive, and easy to operate as possible.
(4) The system should operate during at least one daily recess period and in whichever classroom periods the child's behavior is problematic.
(5) The classroom component should be an individual monitoring and reward system.
(6) The playground component should include the child's peers and earned rewards shared equally with them.

The remainder of this section presents information on the following topics: (1) the classroom behavior management system, (2) the playground behavior management system, (3) procedures for extending the program to other classroom and playground periods, (4) procedures for fading out the behavior management system, and (5) commonly asked questions and answers about the ACCEPTS behavior management system.

The Classrom Behavior Management System

An individual contingency that combines point *earning* and *losing* features is used to strengthen the specific classroom skills taught by the ACCEPTS Curriculum and to reduce or eliminate unacceptable social behavior(s) that interfere with a satisfactory classroom adjustment. Points earned daily during academic periods can be saved and exchanged for special privileges arranged either at school or home.

The Classroom Behavior Management System is introduced just prior to the end of instruction in the ACCEPTS classroom skills. There are a series of sequential steps to follow in setting up the program. They are listed below and then described in greater detail along with guidelines for applying them.

Step One: Identify the academic periods in which the child's behavior is a problem.
Step Two: Select the period(s) in which the program will operate.
Step Three: Review and tailor a list of acceptable/unacceptable behaviors to which the program will apply.
Step Four: Explain and discuss with the target child the point recording form "Things to Do and Things Not to Do" (see Appendix 12).
Step Five: Identify a list of privileges/rewards the child would like to work for.
Step Six: Begin the daily rating of the child's classroom behavior on the last day of instruction in *classroom skills*.

The program should be applied during at least one daily academic period. It can be extended to cover all periods of the instructional day if needed.

The behavior management program should be applied to the four classroom skills taught by the curriculum and to any other adaptive competencies the teacher may be specifically concerned with. A list of unacceptable social behaviors should also be identified that are incompatible with classroom adjustment. Both these lists should be tailored to meet the particular needs of target children and the concerns of their teachers and parents. As a rule, there should be no more than five to seven behaviors in each list, with at least as many adaptive as maladaptive behaviors listed.

A sample listing of behaviors is provided below.

Adaptative Behaviors

- Listen to the teacher
- Do what the teacher says
- Do your best work
- Follow classroom rules
- Let the teacher know you need help the right way
- Listen while others are speaking
- Work on assigned tasks

Maladaptive Behaviors

- Disturb others while they're working
- Talk out of turn
- Don't respond when called upon
- Pay attention to things other than your assignment
- Interrupt the teacher when she/he is busy

Once the lists have been finalized, they should be entered on the point recording form in Appendix 12. This form was designed to provide feedback to the child regarding why points are awarded or lost, and provide a record of the number of points earned daily. The adaptive list should be entered under "Things to Do" and the maladaptive list entered under "Things Not to Do".

A sample rating form with a hypothetical set of ratings is presented below.

In using this form the teacher meets with the target child near the end of each period (or at the end of morning and afternoon sessions for higher functioning children) and provides feedback on the *adaptive* (Things to Do) and *maladaptive* (Things Not to Do) behaviors. If the child has displayed the adaptive behaviors at a minimally acceptable level, a check is placed beside each that meets criterion. Similarly, if the teacher observes one or more instances of the maladaptive items, a check is placed beside each that has been noted. It is important to review the child's status on each behavior on the two lsits.

THINGS TO DO

- Listen while others are speaking
- Let the teacher know you need help in the right way
- Listen carefully to teacher directions and instructions for assignments
- Do what the teacher says
- Follow classroom rules
- Work on assigned tasks

_____

_____

_____

_____

ACADEMIC PERIODS

1	2	3	4	5	6	7
	X		X	X		X
X	X	X		X	X	X
X			X	X	X	X
	X			X		X
X		X		X		X
	X		X	X		

Totals

3	4	2	3	6	2	5

THINGS NOT TO DO

- Pay attention to things other than your assignment
- Disturb others while they're busy or working
- Talk out of turn
- Not repond when called on
- Interrupt the teacher when she/he is busy

_____

_____

_____

_____

ACADEMIC PERIODS

1	2	3	4	5	6	7
X					X	X
	X		X	X		X
						X
		X				
			X	X		

Totals

1	1	1	2	2	1	3

2	3	1	1	4	1	2

NET POINTS EARNED

For low functioning or very disruptive children it may be necessary to convert this form to a frequency recording procedure where each instance of adaptive and maladaptive behavior is noted and recorded as it occurs. Although more demanding for the teacher, some children will require a system variation of this type.

The number of maladaptive behavioral items with checks beside them is subtracted daily from the number of adaptive items with checks beside them and a net total obtained. One point is awarded for each unit of the net difference, e.g., a net difference of five equals five points. If more maladaptive items are checked than adaptive, the net difference is always zero.

Below is a list of possible activity rewards for use with the individual classroom contingency. Along with each activity is a recommended point value to be used as a guide in determining the level of a child's performance required for earning that activity. These values are based on a maximum of 20 points per day or a ½ day program. For a one hour program these values should be divided by three; for a full day program they should be multiplied by two.

Activity	Point Value
Freetime minutes (one half per point)	1 to 20
Crossword puzzle, dot-to-dot, word search	15
Looking at filmstrip	30
Listening to records	20
Game with teacher	35
Classroom helper	40
Soda with principal/counselor	55
Line leader	20
"Rent" on classroom book/game (to take home)	55
Special note home	20
_____	___
_____	___
_____	___

The teacher should discuss the point system in detail with the child before applying it. This discussion should focus on specific competencies- behaviors that earn points (Things to Do), (Things Not to Do) that cause points to be subtracted, and the above list of reward activities and point values. It is most important that the child understand the system completely.

Opportunities should be made available for the child to exchange points for activity rewards daily. Space should be available on the list for the child to contribute items to it and the list should be revised and updated frequently. Whenever possible, home privileges should be built into the list provided that parental cooperation can be obtained.

The Playground Behavior Management System

The ACCEPTS playground behavior management system was designed as a recess incentive program to guarantee the use of newly learned social skills, increase the amount of time the target child and his/her peers play together, and improve the target child's access to organized play activities. The sysem uses a combined individual/group contingency where peers are involved in assisting the target child to meet the reward criterion, and share in earned activity rewards. The system also incorporates intensive coaching procedures and social praise from adults. In implementing the program a 15 to 30 minute recess period (preferably noon or afternoon) should be selected daily during which the target child's *social skills, peer-to-peer interactions,* and *social participation* can be observed, evaluated and reinforced.

Five steps must be carried out before beginning the recess incentive program. These are as follows:

Step One: Select a recess period of at least 15 mintues in length in which primarily child directed free play activities occur.

Step Two: Identify a site and time for freetime activities.

Step Three: Develop a menu of freetime activities.

Step Four: Describe coaching and reinforcement procedures to child.

Step Five: Present incentive program to classmates who will be sharing the recess period.

Someone must assume responsibility for operating the recess program. Ideally, it should be the same person who does the teaching, however, this is not essential to the program's success.

Arrangements must be made for the target child and selected peers to consume earned freetime on a daily basis. The freetime should be made available either immediately after recess or at the end of the day. A site or section of the room should be selected in which freetime activities will not prove disruptive of the ongoing classroom regimen.

Freetime activities should be selected that provide some structure to the freetime period and that are attractive to children. They should also be suitable for groups of two to four children at a time and provide for cooperative exchanges.

Below is a suggested list of activities that teachers could provide during the daily freetime for the target child and selected peers. These activities meet the above criteria and should take several days to complete. When the activity or project is completed, a brief freetime activity should be arranged for the *entire* class (Details of this procedure will be discussed later).

SUGGESTED ACTIVITY REWARDS

Puzzles — put together or crossword
Paint/draw a mural
  Suggestion:
    Of kids in your class
    Of kids playing together on playground
    Seasonal type —
      Halloween scene
      Pilgrims
      Christmas scene, etc.
Collage — magazine cutouts
Paint/color by number
Paper mache
Weaving — basket or wall hanging
Stitchery — potholders/wallhanging/hook rug
Soap carving
Models
Word search
Dot-to-Dot

_____

_____

_____

_____

Details of the recess incentive system should be explained to and discussed with the target child in the same way that the classroom system was presented. The material to be described below on the operation of the system should be studied carefully before making this presentation.

Finally, the coach and target child present the program to classmates who will be sharing the recess period and explain their role in it. A sample script is provided below to assist you in making this presentation. This is only a sample and you are free to change it as your preferences dictate.

Presentation to Class

"*Hi. My name is* _____. I work on a program that is trying to find ways of teaching children how to talk, play, and make new friends. We are asking some boys and girls to help out by trying the program with us. _____ has agreed to help us, but I'm going to need your help, too. Everybody has to participate to make our program work.

"Here's how you can help. During recess (identify which recess) _____ will be able to earn freetime for talking and playing in a friendly way with the children in this class. During recess I will watch how _____ plays and which of you boys and girls play with him/her. Then, at the end of recess, I will pick a couple of people who played with _____ and they will get to share his/her freetime. Then, every few days, when everyone has been helping out and _____ is earning lots of freetime, there will be special activities for the whole class! How does that sound? Any questions?

"Now let's talk about what you can do to help _____ earn freetime. One way you can help is by asking him/her to play with you. What kinds of games could you ask _____ to play? What else could you do to help _____ earn freetime?" (Elicit discussion which suggests ways which would encourage the target child to play and earn points).

Finally, tell the students when you will begin the recess program and thank them for listening.

A recess rating form is used to deliver the program during recess periods. A copy of this form is contained in Appendix 13. The form makes it possible to evaluate the target child's social behavior, to provide feedback, and to award earned freetime minutes. Go to Appendix 13 and study the form carefully before proceeding further.

Points are awarded for three elements of the child's social behavior during recess. First, the child's rate or degree of *social participation* is evaluated by: (1) dividing the recess into successive five-minute periods (that is, a 15 minute recess would be divided into three five-minute periods), and (2) at the end of each period, judging whether the child has participated in a positive way with peers for at least *half* of the five minute segment. If the child did participate, a "yes" is circled on the rating form. If not, a "no" is circled. Second, three specific *social skills* are listed on the rating form each day. The two most recently taught social skills and one review skill are listed daily. The child is awarded one minute of freetime for using each skill correctly during recess. Finally, at the end of recess the coach judges the child's overall *skill level* in displaying the three focus skills. This rating, ranging from 1 (low skills performance) to 5 (highly skilled) is noted on the record sheet and one minute of freetime is awarded for each point, e.g., a rating of 3 equals three minutes of earned freetime.

In addition to awarding points, the teacher (or other professional) provides direct coaching to the child during a selected recess period. Coaching assists the child in developing new skills by providing intensive, individually tailored instruction during ongoing recess periods. Coaching in the ACCEPTS program includes three components. These are: Prompting, priming, and praising. *Prompting* involves meeting briefly with the child prior to (or occasionally, during) recess to review skills that help make friends, and help the child plan *what* to play and *whom* to play with. The coach *primes* the child to play during recess by suggesting specific activities to join or peers to interact with. *Priming* is applied when the target child is not interacting with others, or fails to display a specific social skill when it is called for. *Priming* serves as a form of direct instruction in the timing and appropriate use of social skills. *Praising* peer-to-peer interactions and the appropriate use of social skills is perhaps the most important part of coaching. The target child should receive positive, descriptive social praise: (1) *during* recess for the use of appropriate skills, and (2) at the *end* of recess, for overall performance. In the early stages of the program, the target child should be praised frequently (e.g., during or following each successful social interaction). Later, the frequency and intensity of praise can be reduced somewhat. Consult Appendix 11 for a list of descriptive praises.

The coach should keep a running tally of the number of children the target child interacts with during recess. Notes should also be kept on the degree to which they are facilitative of the target child's social participation. This information will be used to select a small number of peers to share freetime with the target child.

During freetime, these children are assigned to work on some semi-structured activity or project such as completing a puzzle, building something, or painting a mural of some type. The project may require anywhere from two days to a week to finish at a rate of 8 to 10 minutes daily. When the activity is finished, a special freetime activity reward is made available to the whole class. In this way the target child is motivated to socially participate, specific children are rewarded on a daily basis for playing with the target child, and the peer group is occasionally rewarded for being supportive of the child's social participation.

Inclusion of the target child's classmates is critically important for at least two reasons. First, if the amount of time peers spend playing/interacting with the target child is increased we have also increased the number of opportunities the child has to practice newly acquired skills and to be reinforced for doing so. Second, it is important to change the behavior and attitudes of the target child's peers. Classmates often have a long history of socially punishing and/or ignoring the target child's unskilled attempts at social participation. Given this history, peers frequently have to be encouraged, prompted, and praised for interacting with him or her.

At the end of the recess period, the coach and target child should meet briefly to assess performance and tally the number of freetime minutes earned. This feedback process should cover the following topics: (1) discuss the number of freetime minutes earned for social participation, the focus social skills, and the overall skill level, (2) praise the child for positive/skilled aspects of his/her behavior, and (3) point out what could have been done to earn additional freetime minutes if the maximum was not earned.

A point record form is provided in Appendix 14 for keeping track of both classroom points and freetime minutes earned daily. It is provided for your convenience only and is not a required part of the program.

If possible, the coach and target child should meet immediately after recess with the child's class to announce the amount of freetime earned and the peers who were selected to share in the earned freetime. If a number of peers "qualify" to share freetime, a smaller group can be chosen randomly. The authors have put peers' names on slips of paper and had the target child pick two or three from a box — everyone seems to enjoy this "game."

The daily steps required to operate the recess incentive system are presented below:
These steps repeat daily for as long as the fully intact recess incentive system is in effect.

One of the outcomes of the recess program is usually an increase in the amount of time the target child interacts with peers. Prior research experience of the senior author indicates that in rare cases some children's social behavior becomes increasingly negative as it increases. If this should happen with the ACCEPTS program, a response cost procedure will effectively control it in most cases. Simply inform the child of the problem, describe or role play instances of it, and subtract ½

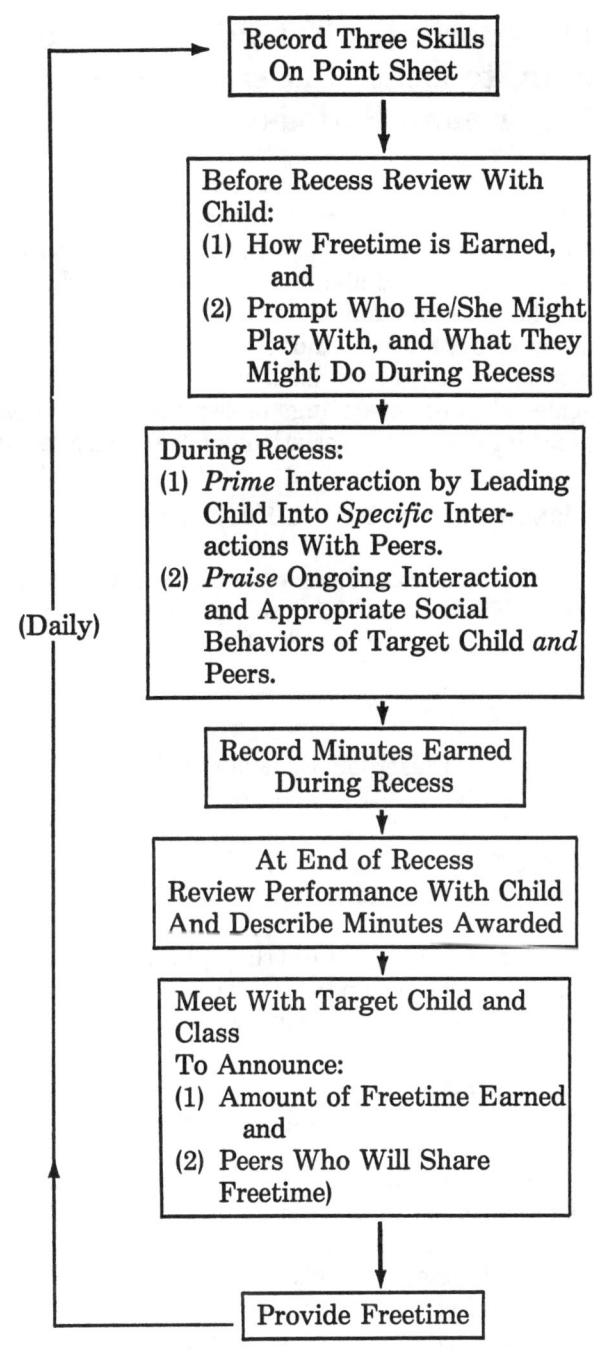

or 1 minute of freetime each time an instance occurs. An immediate reduction or in rate of negative behavior should occur.

Procedures for Extending the Program to Other Classroom and Playground Periods

The most direct way to extend the behavior management program to other classroom and recess periods is to implement the systems within them as described above. However, this will often not be feasible and only the most deficient or disruptive children would require this level of intervention. Substantial behavioral impact can be achieved in other settings or periods via low cost procedures that are variations of the full program.

Classroom Extension Procedures.

The authors recommend that the form illustrated below be used for this purpose (A copy is also contained in Appendix 15).

ACCEPTS
Classroom Behavior Daily
Rating Form

Child's Name _____ Date _____
Teacher _____

Instructions: Please rate the appropriateness of the child's classroom behavior on a scale of 1 to 5 during designated academic periods.

Inappropriate   *Appropriate*
    1......2......3......4......5

Please use the following list of appropriate classroom behaviors as criteria in making your rating:

(1) Listening to instructions and directions
(2) Making assistance needs known
(3) Producing work of acceptable quality.
(4) Following established classroom rules
(5) Complying with teacher instructions/commands

If the child complied with these criteria during the rating period, he/she should receive a high rating. If not, then a lower rating should be given. Explain the rating to the child and provide verbal praise for good performance. Write a brief comment about good performance when the child receives a rating of 3 or higher.

The child behaviors listed on this form define satisfactory adjustment or behavioral performance in most classrooms. All of them are addressed by the ACCEPTS classroom skills instructional content.

The authors have used this form extensively. Teachers find it easy to use and effective in communicating information regarding the child's behavioral status.

In using the form to extend the program to other class periods, the child's behavior is rated on it by the teacher or supervisor in that setting. The form is returned to the primary teacher and the rating given multiplied times either .5 or 1 (depending on preference) to determine the number of points earned. These points are added to the child's cumulative point total. This procedure can be reported for all periods in which the program is to be extended.

Recess Extension Procedures.

As with the classroom program, the recess incentive system could simply be applied as is in other periods. For very deficient children, this may be necessary. Whenever possible, however, less involved procedures should be used.

In prior research with socially withdrawn children, the senior author and his colleagues (Hops, Walker, & Greenwood, 1979) successfully used the following procedure to extend a recess intervention program to other recess periods. It consisted of three components: (1) a verbal contracting procedure, (2) a self report procedure, and (3) adult praise and proved to be highly effective in producing behavior changes in non-intervention recess periods.

After the original intervention program was established and working well in the primary recess period, the extension procedure was introduced. Each day the teacher assigned a different peer to play with the target child in the other recess periods. The teacher held a brief review session before the recess and asked what games/activities they were going to play, and which other children, if any, they planned to include. After each recess period the teacher held a debriefing session and reviewed the recess periods and the activities engaged in. Praise was used liberally to support the child's attempts at social participation in other recesses.

The authors recommend the following variation of this procedure for extending the ACCEPTS recess incentive program to other periods. It is divided into three sequential stages.

Stage One
(1) Assign a different peer each day to play with the target child in other recesses.
(2) Use the reviewing and debriefing procedures before and after recess as described above.
(3) Award the two children several minutes of freetime each if they played together as planned *if other children in the recess period verify their self reports.*
(4) Praise both children's performance.

Once this procedure is developed and working well, shift to Stage Two.

Stage Two
(1) Select a peer to verify the target child's self report *before* recess.
(2) Use reviewing and debriefing procedures with the target child daily.
(3) Interview peer to verify target child's self report.
(4) If accurate, praise and award a good day card to send home that can count toward a home privilege of some type.

Shift to Stage Three when the child has adjusted to the program and when peer reports consistently verify the target child's accounts of social participation.

Stage Three
(1) use reviewing and debriefing periods with the target child as before.
(2) Praise reports of social contact with peers and active social participation.

If implemented as described, this overall program will have a substantial impact on the child's level of social participation in other recess periods. It is recommended that the teacher or coach observe occasionally in these recess periods to provide an additional basis for verifying target child and peer reports.

Procedures for Fading the ACCEPTS Behavior Management Systems

Systematic procedures are described below for gradually fading out the classroom and playground behavior management programs. There are no hard and fast rules governing the fading process. The procedures outlined below are but one way of accomplishing this task and are presented for the teacher's consideration. These procedures were implemented by the authors in developing and testing the ACCEPTS program and were found to be successful in preserving behavioral gains while fading out program components.

There seems to be almost universal agreement among school professionals regarding the importance of systematic fading procedures. The ultimate goal of this process is to transfer control of the behavior change and maintenance process to the target child.

The history of behavioral intervention procedures and programs indicates that behavioral gains quickly deteriorate if powerful contingency management systems are abruptly terminated. Walker (1979) has argued that behavior change is a two-stage process consisting of a set of procedures that produce behavior change and a second set of procedure that maintain achieved gains over the long term. Fading procedures are an extremely important part of stage two.

The classroom and playground fading procedures below are designed for the gradual removal of program components in the *primary* classroom and recess periods in which the full program has been implemented. Fading should not be initiated until the instructional process has been completed *and* the behavior management procedures have stabilized the target child's behavior at acceptable levels.

Fading the Classroom Behavior Management System

Fading of the classroom system should be considered when the child's appropriate classroom behavior is consistently at 80% or better. Fading of the classroom contingency is a relatively easy task since the child's behavior is already under the control of the appropriate adult — the classroom teacher.

Fading involves three steps over a seven week period. These are:

(1) Reducing the frequency or occasions on which backup rewards are available.
(2) Curtailing use of the point recording form.
(3) Shifting to a natural feedback system involving regular debriefings and social praise. A suggested fading schedule is provided below.

Week of Fading	Point Record Form Completed	Backup Awards Available
One	Daily	M, W, F
Two	Daily	W, F
Three	Over 3 Days	W, F
Four	Over 3 Days	F
Five	Over 5 Days	F
Six	Over 5 Days	Intermittent
Seven	Intermittent	Intermittent

As the fading schedule progresses, it is *extremely important* that the teacher maintain a high level of social praise and use debriefing procedures regularly. The focus of debriefing should be on providing objective feedback regarding the child's classroom behavior, e.g., for On-Task and Appropriate behavior. The speed of fading should be tailored to the individual child so that acceptable rates of behavior are maintained.

Fading the Recess Incentive Program

The specifics of the fading plan will vary from school to school and child to child depending upon how the recess period is structured and the extent to which the cooperation of recess supervisors can be obtained.

Fading should not begin until the target child is consistently interacting and/or socially participating at 90% or better of the available recess time. Four major tasks must be accomplished in fading the recess incentive program. These are:

(1) Reducing the coach's role in directly prompting and priming the child's social behavior.
(2) Increasing the recess supervisor's role in the program.
(3) Increasing teacher involvement.
(4) Developing a schedule for fading the Recess Rating Form and Freetime Activity Rewards.

Each of these tasks is described below.

Reducing the Coach's Role

The coach should begin fading *physical proximity*, the *rate of prompts*, and the *amount of social praise* provided during the recess period. After several weeks of fading, the coach's interaction with the target child should ideally consist of (1) a *brief* session at the beginning of recess to ask what the child is going to do during recess, (2) two or three "callouts" for continued interaction during recess, and (3) a brief session at the end of recess to review the child's performance.

At this point, the child should not rely (to any great extent) on the coach to maintain appropriate interaction and social participation. The before recess conference should be a chance for the child to tell how he/she will spend recess. The coach should praise any plan that leads to appropriate interaction (such as "I'm going to play with Sarah" or "I'm going to play soccer").

As you reduce your direct support and involvement in the program and increase your physical distance from the child and your rate of social reinforcement, you will be behaving more like the adult supervising the recess — the person the target child should begin responding to. This is also a time to model monitoring and praising the child for the supervisor. As you move away from the child, begin to spend more time near/with the supervisor. During recess, as the child continues to interact appropriately with peers, deliver several "callout" praises from the edge of the child's activity or from across the playground. Call the child and *quickly* praise — "Hey Shannon, looks like you're having fun!" (Initially, you may have to intersperse some closer contact. Later, these callouts can be as simple as getting the child's attention, smiling, and giving an "OK" sign).

At the end of the recess period ask the child how they thought recess went, praise accurate reports, briefly provide your own evaluation, and give the point sheet to the child to deliver to the teacher.

Increasing the Recess Supervisor's Role

As responsibility for operating the program shifts to the recess supervisor, there will be a change in how the child's behavior is evaluated. The coach should implement this revised procedure the last two days before leaving the playground, and train the supervisor in its use.

The form that supervisors will use is a simplified version of the Recess Rating Form used by the coach (see Appendix 16 for a copy). It requires that supervisors monitor the child's behavior four times during recess, and rate the overall quality of the child's interaction at the end of recess. To monitor the child's behavior the supervisor divides the recess into four approximately equal periods, and at the *end* of each interval, briefly observes the child. If, at that time, the child is engaged in appropriate interaction, a "+" is awarded; if not, a "—". To rate the quality of interaction, recess supervisors should informally monitor the type of activities the child participates in, and the quality of his/her interaction in those activities. The supervisor evaluates the child's overall skill level on a scale of 0 to 5 with 5 representing maximally skilled performance.

The recess supervisor also meets with the child at the end of recess, briefly giving specific details of why points were awarded/not awarded. Additionally, the supervisor should provide two or three "callout" praises during recess. The recess supervisor's program duties can be incorporated into their ongoing activities quite easily. However, it is important for you to monitor their performance and to provide assistance and support as needed.

Increasing Teacher Involvement

During the fading process it is important for the child's teacher to assume a more active role in the program. Teacher demands in this regard are held to an absolute minimum.

The teacher's primary responsibility is to (1) provide point sheets to the child *before* recess, for delivery to the recess supervisor, (2) collect the point sheet and deliver social praise immediately after recess, and (3) provide freetime. In this phase the child will earn *five minutes* of free time if *both* of the following criteria are met: interact with peers 75% of the monitored time (i.e., three of the four checks), *and* maintain an overall skill level rating of 3 or higher.

Fading Schedule for the Point Recording Form and Freetime Rewards

After the target child has adjusted to the new rating form and to the recess supervisor's operation of the program (e.g., his/her behavioral level has stabilized), a schedule should be implemented to gradually fade out the form and freetime rewards. A suggested schedule is provided below. However, the child's fading program should be moved only as rapidly as he/she continues to maintain rates of 75% of appropriate interaction and overall skill level ratings of 3 or higher.

Week of Fading	Point Sheets	Freetime
One	Daily	Daily
Two	1 each 2 days	T, Th, F
Three	Mon-Tues/Wed-Fri.	T, F
Four	Mon-Thurs/None Fri	
Five	None Mon-Tues/One Wed-Fri	
Six	None	
Seven	None	

Commonly Asked Questions and Answers About the ACCEPTS Behavior Management System

In developing and field testing the ACCEPTS program a number of questions about the behavior management system were repeatedly encountered. These questions and the responses to them are listed below.

— WHO SHOULD COACH?

The teacher who does the instruction is ideal. Other possibilities are the school psychologist, counselor, or aide.

— WHICH PEER GROUP SHOULD BE INCLUDED

If the target child is being mainstreamed, the regular class peers should be included. If not, then handicapped classmates in the special education setting. A third option is volunteer helpers drawn from several classrooms.

— WHAT TYPES OF REWARDS SHOULD BE USED?

It is highly recommended that freetime rewards and special privileges at school and home be used. Tangible rewards (toys, edibles, etc.) should be avoided if at all possible.

— HOW CAN PEERS BE MOTIVATED TO PLAY WITH THE TARGET CHILD?

The playground contingency encourages peer group members to include the target child and to play with him/her. Selected peers share freetime rewards with the target child. The coach should also prompt peers to play with the target child at recess.

— WHAT IF IT ISN'T POSSIBLE TO COACH DAILY?

Coaching should occur daily, if possible. Other possibilities include using older, more competent peers as "helpers" on off days. This would require some training in prompting, praising, and coaching. Another possibility is to have the playground supervisor monitor the child, provide minimal feedback. and complete a *single* rating of quality of social interaction at the end of recess.

— PEERS FLOCK AROUND THE TARGET CHILD AND PLAY DOES NOT SEEM NATURAL!

Be patient. This is a typical response during the early parts of the program. In time, fewer peers seek the child's attention and play is more natural.

REFERENCES

Allen, K.E., Benning, P.M., & Drummond, T.W. Integration of normal and handicapped children in a behavior modification preschool: A case study. In G. Semb (Ed.), *Behavior analysis and education*. Lawrence, Kansas: University of Kansas Press, 1972.

Asher, S., & Taylor, A. Social outcomes of mainstreaming: Sociometric assessment and beyond. *Aspen Systems Corporation*, 1981, 13-30.

Ballard, M., Corman, L., Gottlieb, J., & Kaufman, M.J. Improving the social status of mainstreamed retarded children. *Journal of Educational Psychology*, 1978, 69, 605-611.

Barclay, J. Interest patterns associated with measures of social desirability. *Personality Guidance Journal*, 1966, 45, 56-60.

Becker, W. *Parents are teachers*. Champaign, IL: Research Press, 1971.

Brophy, J.E., & Good, T. Teachers' communication of differential expectations for children's classroom performance: Some behavioral data. *Journal of Educational Psychology*, 1970, 61, 365-374.

Brophy, J.E., & Good, T. *Teacher-student relationships: Causes and consequences*. New York: Holt, Rinehart and Winston, 1974.

Bruininks, V.L. Peer status and personality characteristics of learning disabled and nondisabled students. *Journal of Learning Disabilities*, 1978, 11, 484-489.

Bruininks, R., Rynders, J., & Gross, J. Social acceptance of mildly retarded pupils in resource rooms and regular classes. *American Journal of Mental Deficiency*, 1974, 78, 377-383.

Bryan, T.S. Peer popularity of learning disabled children. *Journal of Learning Disabilities*, 1974, 7, 621-625.

Bryan, T.S. Peer popularity of learning disabled children: A replication. *Journal of Learning Disabilities*, 1976, 9, 307-311.

Bryan, T.S. Social relationships and verbal interactions of learning disabled children. *Journal of Learning Disabilities*, 1978, 11, 107-115.

Bryan, T.S., & Wheeler, R. Perception of children with learning disabilities: The eye of the observer. *Journal of Learning Disabilities*, 1972, 5, 484-488.

Carnine, D., & Silbert, J. *Direct instruction: Reading*. Columbus, Ohio: Charles Merrill, 1980.

Cowen, E.L., Pederson, A., Babigan, H., Izzo, L.D., & Trost, M.A. Long-term follow-up of early detected vulnerable children. *Journal of Consulting and Clinical Psychology*, 1973, 41, 438-446.

Dwiggins, D. An investigation of differences in teacher standards and expectations that teachers hold for handicapped versus non-handicapped students. Doctoral dissertation, University of Oregon, August 1981.

Feitelson, D., Weintraub, S., & Michael, O. Social interactions in heterogenous preschools in Israel. *Child Development*, 1972, 43, 1, 249-259.

Foster, S.L., & Ritchey, W.L. Issues in the assessment of social competence in children. *Journal of Applied Behavior Analysis*, 1979, 12, 625-638.

Goodman, H., Gottlieb, J., & Harrison, R. Social acceptance of EMRs integrated into a nongraded elementary school. *American Journal of Mental Deficiency*, 1972, 76, 412-417.

Gottlieb, J. Attitudes toward retarded children: Effects of labeling and behavioral aggressiveness. *Journal of Educational Psychology*, 1975, *67*, 581-585.

Gottlieb, J. Placement in the least restrictive environment. In *LRE: Developing criteria for the evaluation of the least restrictive environment provision*. Philadelphia, PA: Research for Better Schools, 1979.

Gottlieb, J., & Budoff, M. Social acceptability of retarded children in nongraded schools differing in architecture. *American Journal of Mental Deficiency*, 1973, *78*, 15-19.

Gottman, J., Gonso, J., & Rasmussen, B. Social interaction, social competence, and friendship in children. *Child Development*, 1975, *46*, 709-718.

Gresham, F. Social skills training with handicapped children: A review. *Review of Educational Research*, 1981, *51*(1), 139-176.

Gresham, F. Misguided mainstreaming: The case for social skills training with handicapped children. *Exceptional Children*, 1982, *48*, 422-433.

Guralnick, M. Integrated preschools as educational and therapeutic environments. In M. Guralnick (Ed.), *Early intervention and the integration of handicapped and nonhandicapped children*. Baltimore: University Park Press, 1978.

Guralnick, M. Programmatic factors affecting child-child social interactions in mainstreamed preschool programs. *Exceptional Educational Quarterly*, 1981, *1*, 71-91.

Hartup, W. Peer relations and the growth of social competence. In M.W. Kent & J.E. Rolf (Eds.). *Primary prevention of psychopathology (Vol. 3): Social competence in children*. Hanover, NH: University Press of New England, 1979.

Hops, H. Social skills training for socially isolated children. In P. Karoly & J.M. Steffen (Eds.), *Advances in child behavior analysis and therapy (Vol. 2): Intellectual and social deficiencies*. New York: Gardner Press, in press.

Hops, H., Walker, H.M., & Greenwood, C.R. PEERS: A program for remediating social withdrawal in school. Behavioral systems for the developmentally disabled. In L.A. Hamerlynck (Ed.), *School and family environments*. New York: Bruner/Mazel, 1979.

Kazdin, A.E. Assessing the clinical or applied importance of behavior change through social validation. *Behavior Modification*, 1977, *1*, 427-452.

Keogh, B., & Levitt, M. Special education in the mainstream: A confrontation of limitations. Focus on *Exceptional Children*, 1976, *8*, 1-10.

La Greca, A. Children's social skills: An overview. Guest editorial for a special issue of *Pediatric Psychology* on children's social skills, 1981, *4*, 335-341.

La Greca, A., & Mesibov, G. Social skills intervention with learning disabled children: Selecting skills and implementing training. *Journal of Clinical Child Psychology*, 1979, *8*, 234-241.

La Greca, A., & Santogrossi, D. Social skills training with elementary school students: A behavioral group approach. *Journal of Consulting and Clinical Psychology*, 1980, *48*, 220-227.

Laughlin, F. *The peer status of six and seventh grade children*. Bureau of Publications. Teachers College, Columbia University, 1954.

MacMillan, D., Jones, R., & Meyers, C. Mainstreaming the mildly retarded: Some questions, cautions, and guidelines. *Mental Retardation*, 1976, February 3-10.

Michelson, L., & Wood, R. Behavioral assessment and training of children's social skills. *Progress in Behavior Modification*, 1980, *9*, 241-291.

Milburn, J., & Cartledge, G. The how-to of effective social skills teaching. *The Directive Teacher*, Winter 1981, p. 12.

Miller, W. *Systematic Parent Training*. Champaign, IL: Research Press, 1975.

Morgan, S.R. A descriptive analysis of maladjusted behavior in socially rejected children. *Behavioral Disorders*, 1977, *3*, 23-30.

Muma, J. Peer evaluation and academic performance. *Personality Guidance Journal*, 1965, *44*, 405-409.

Muma, J. Peer evaluation and academic achievement in performance classes. *Personality Guidance Journal*, 1968, *46*, 580-585.

Pekarik, E.G., Printz, R.J., Liebert, D.E., Weintraub, S., & Neale, J.M. The pupil evaluation inventory: A Sociometric technique for assessing children's social behavior. *Journal of Abnormal Child Psychology*, 1976, *4*, 83-97.

Ray, J.S. Behavior of developmentally delayed and non-delayed toddler-age children: An ethological study. Unpublished doctoral dissertation, George Peabody College, 1974.

Roff, M. Childhood social interactions and young adult bad conduct. *Journal of Abnormal Social Psychology*, 1961, *63*, 333-337.

Roff, M., Sells, B., & Golden, M. *Social adjustment and personality development in children*. Minneapolis: University of Minnesota Press, 1972.

Sarason, S., & Doris, J. Mainstreaming: Dilemmas, opposition, opportunities. Chapter in M. Reynolds, (Ed.), *Futures of education for exceptional children: Emerging structures*. Reston: Council for Exceptional Children, 1978.

Stephens, T. Teaching social behavior: The schools' challenge in the 1980s. *The Directive Teacher*, Winter 1981, 1-4.

Stokes, T., & Baer, D. An implicit technology of generalization. *Journal of Applied Behavior Analysis*, 1977, *10*, No. 2, 349-358.

Van Hasselt, V.B., Hersen, M., Whitehill, M.D., & Bellack, A.S. *Social skills assessment and training for children: An evaluative review*. Behavior Research and Therapy, 1979, *17*, 413-437.

Victor, J.B., & Halverson, C.F. Behavior problems in elementary school children: A follow-up study. *Journal of Abnormal Child Psychology*, 1976, *4*, 17-29.

Walker, H.M. *The acting out child: Coping with classroom disruption*. Boston: Allyn & Bacon, 1979.

Walker, H.M., Hops, H., & Greenwood, C.R. The CORBEH research and development model: Programmatic issues and strategies. In S. Paine, T. Bellamy, and B. Wilcox (Eds.), Baltimore: Paul H. Brookes Publishing Co. In press.

Walker, H.M., McConnell, S., Walker, J., Clarke, J., Todis, B., Cohen, G., & Rankin, R. Initial analysis of the ACCEPTS curriculum: Efficacy of instructional and behavior management procedures for improving the social adjustment of handicapped children. *Analysis and intervention in developmental disabilities*. In press.

APPENDICES

APPENDIX 1: Overview of the SBS (Social Behavior Survival) Program 119

APPENDIX 2: ACCEPTS Reference List 121

APPENDIX 3: ACCEPTS Teacher Questionnaire 123

APPENDIX 4: Consumer Satisfaction Ratings of the ACCEPTS Curriculum and Behavior Management System 127

APPENDIX 5: Summary: Consumer Satisfaction Ratings of 157 School Professionals Trained in How to Use the ACCEPTS Program 130

APPENDIX 6: ACCEPTS Screening Checklist 132

APPENDIX 7: The ACCEPTS Observation Form 133

APPENDIX 8: ACCEPTS Placement Test 136

APPENDIX 9: ACCEPTS Placement Test Summary Sheet 140

APPENDIX 10: Descriptions of the ACCEPTS Video Scenes for Use in Modeling Positive and Negative Examples 142

APPENDIX 11: Sample Praise Statements 147

APPENDIX 12: Points Recording Form 148

APPENDIX 13: ACCEPTS Recess Rating Form 149

APPENDIX 14: Form for Recording and Tracking Earned Classroom Points and Freetime Minutes at Recess 152

APPENDIX 15: Classroom Behavior Daily Rating Form 153

APPENDIX 16: ACCEPTS Recess Rating Form 154

APPENDIX I

Overview of the SBS (*Social Behavior Survival*) Program

Program Goals

The SBS Program focuses on the placement and integration components of P.L. 94-142 and is designed primarily for handicapped children in grades K-6 and their teachers. Specifically, the program's major goals are: (1) To select appropriate placement settings for the integration of mildly and moderately handicapped children into the educational mainstream, and (2) to prepare such children (a) to meet the receiving teacher's behavior expectations, and (b) to achieve adjustment to non-handicapped peer groups.

Program Components

The SBS Program has two major components: assessment and intervention. Together they make it possible to assess the behavioral demands and expectations of less restrictive settings and to systematically prepare the mainstream handicapped child to cope with them prior to actual integration.

Assessment. The assessment component, AIMS (*A*ssessments for *I*ntegration into *M*ainstream *S*ettings) is designed for use in: (1) The selection of mainstream settings, (2) identifying the adaptive skills and competencies required in the receiving setting, as well as maladaptive social behavior judged unacceptable by the receiving teacher, (3) providing information on the receiving teacher's technical assistance needs in teaching and managing the mainstreamed child.

AIMS provides an ecological assessment of potential mainstream settings and relies upon teacher ratings of adaptive and maladaptive classes of child behavior. Direct observational methods are used to assess the handicapped child's adjustment to such settings following integration. The AIMS system contains the following instruments:
— The SBS Inventory of Teacher Social Behavior Standards and Expectations.
— The SBS Checklist of Correlates of Child Handicapping Conditions.
— The Social Interaction Code.
— The Classroom Adjustment Code.

Intervention. The social skills training program called ACCEPTS (*A C*urriculum for *C*hildren's *Ef*fective *P*eer and *T*eacher *S*kills) is used to teach critically important teacher and peer-to-peer behavioral competencies essential for a successful adjustment to the behavioral demands of mainstream settings. The ACCEPTS program contains the following elements:
— A nine-step instructional procedure based on principles of direct instruction.
— Scripts for teaching four critically important teacher-child behavioral competencies and twenty-four peer-to-peer social skills.
— Videotaped examples and non-examples of the skills being taught.
— Behavior management procedures for use during the teaching process and for strengthening correct applications of the skills in playground and classroom settings.
— Guidelines for using the curriculum and for training others to accept it.

School Applications

The AIMS system and ACCEPTS curriculum were designed for use in the mainstreaming process. In combination they provide an integrated assessment-intervention approach to some of the problems encountered in the integration of handicapped children into less restrictive settings. However, the two components can be used independently of each other.

Additional program applications would include:

For AIMS
(1) Determining the inservice needs of regular and special education teachers in the area of behavior management.
(2) Providing a basis for assigning teachers to students and vice versa.
(3) Identifying adaptive skills and competencies judged essential (across teachers) for a successful classroom adjustment.

For ACCEPTS
(1) Teaching critically important peer-to-peer social skills to entire classes of pupils in order to improve overall social competence and to facilitate acceptance of mainstreamed handicapped children.
(2) Improving the appropriate behavior levels of both nonhandicapped and handicapped groups of pupils.

APPENDIX 2

ACCEPTS REFERENCE LIST

AREA I. CLASSROOM SKILLS

	Curriculum Page #	# on ½" Videotape	# on ¾" Videotape
1. Listening to the Teacher	33	008	050
2. When the Teacher Asks You to Do Something	35	020	102
3. Doing Your Best Work	36	041	188
4. Following Classroom Rules	38		
AREA I REVIEW	41		

AREA II. BASIC INTERACTION SKILLS

1. Eye Contact	42		
2. Using the Right Voice	44	053	235
3. Starting	46	059	259
4. Listening	49	074	311
5. Answering	51	086	349
6. Making Sense	53	099	393
7. Taking Turns Talking	55	109	424
8. A Question	58	124	470
9. Continuing	60	135	503
AREA II REVIEW	62		

AREA III. GETTING ALONG SKILLS

1. Using Polite Words	64		
2. Sharing	67	145	532
3. Following Rules	69	155	559
4. Assisting Others	71	166	592
5. Touching the Right Way	74		
AREA III REVIEW	77		

AREA IV. MAKING FRIENDS SKILLS

	Curriculum Page #	# on ½" Videotape	# on ¾" Videotape
1. Good Grooming	78	177	621
2. Smiling	80	182	635
3. Complimenting	82	190	654
4. Friendship Making	84	197	674
AREA IV REVIEW	87		

AREA V. COPING SKILLS

1. When Someone Says "No"	88	203	689
2. When You Express Anger	91	218	729
3. When Someone Teases You	93	231	760
4. When Someone Tries to Hurt You	95	244	794
5. When Someone Asks You to Do Something You Can't Do	97	251	812
6. When Things Don't Go Right	99		
AREA V REVIEW	101		

APPENDIX 3

ACCEPTS TEACHER QUESTIONNAIRE

This brief questionnaire is designed to solicit your input regarding procedures needed to effectively integrate handicapped children into less restrictive settings. The information you provide us will be of great value in designing an instructional package that will be relevant to the needs of teachers of handicapped children. Thank you for your time.

SECTION I — SIGNIFICANCE OF THE PROBLEM

1. Do you see the social skills deficits and maladaptive behaviors that many handicapped children display as being major barriers to effective mainstreaming?
   __21__Yes __2__No _____Unsure

2. Do you think teachers in receiving settings would respond positively to a mainstreaming strategy that (a) identified their specific social behavior standards and then (b) attempted to prepare handicapped children to meet these standards prior to integration?
   __22__Yes _____No __2__Unsure

3. Would a strategy of this type be of value to you as a teacher of handicapped children who participates in the placement/integration process?
   __23__Yes _____No _____Unsure

4. Assuming that a strategy of this type would consume 15 to 20 hours of your time per handicapped child (who was to be mainstreamed) over a two-three month period, would you see it as time well spent?
   __18__Yes _____No __2__Unsure

   4a. Would you be willing to use an instructional package in a one-to-one or small group teaching situation designed to teach handicapped children social skills and adaptive classroom behaviors?
   __22__Yes _____No _____Unsure

   4b. Would you be most comfortable using an instructional package of this type alone or would you prefer to use it only in conjunction with a teacher consultant, e.g., school psychologist, school counselor, or others who provide resource support.

   1. _____Alone
   2. __2__With a teacher consultant only
   3. __19__Either one

5. Do you think it is necessary to track handicapped children into mainstream settings and insure that they can actually exhibit previously mastered skills/competencies in the new setting?
   __24__ Yes _____ No _____ Unsure

6. Will you be given primary responsibility for insuring that mainstreaming works for a given child?
   __15__ Yes __3__ No __6__ Unsure

SECTION II — CHARACTERISTICS/FEATURES OF THE INSTRUCTIONAL PACKAGE

(The questions below are intended to obtain information which will allow us to design a package that will be of maximum value and use to teachers like yourself).

Please check options below that you would like to see incorporated into an instructional package of this type. You are free to check more than one option under each area.

1. Procedures for teaching social skills and adaptive behaviors

   __23__ verbal instructions   __22__ feedback

   __14__ cues   __17__ rewards (points, praise, privileges)

   __15__ prompts   __18__ modeling

   __20__ role play/behavioral rehearsal __8__ homework assignments

2. Organization of package: How should strategies for instruction be categorized in the package?

   __10__ by specific behavior to be taught, eliminated, or decreased (hits, yells, talk-outs, does not comply, etc.)

   __8__ by teaching procedure (verbal instructions, cues, role play, feedback, etc.)

   __17__ by generic groupings of behaviors/skills to be taught (making friends, cooperation, prosocial behavior, aggression, etc.)

   __9__ by intervention setting (special classroom, resource room, regular classroom gym, etc.)

   __11__ by specific behaviors in the order in which they should be mastered.

   _____ via examples presented in case studies

3. Presentation Format

   __22__ detailed, sequenced scripts for use in the instructional process

   __10__ outlines of key areas to cover during instruction

       __5__ lesson plans in paragraph form

       __14__ flow charts on instructional steps

       _____ other, please specify

4. Would you prefer a package that relies primarily upon

   a. __20__ direct or

   b. __1__ non-direct instructional procedures?

5. Which of the teaching situations below would you prefer?

   a. __1__ one-to-one teaching involving you and the handicapped child

   b. __21__ small group instruction involving the handicapped child and either handicapped or non-handicapped peers

   c. __1__ other, please specify

6. Organization of teaching strategies

       __12__ task analyses of each target bahavior

       __15__ specific instructional objectives for each target behavior

       __15__ specific criteria for achievement of objectives

       __18__ sequences to follow for shaping target behaviors

       __10__ scope and sequence (including a task analysis and objectives for each target behavior) in a separate section of the manual

7. Materials for supplementing teacher-led instruction

       __11__ audiotape instructions

       __20__ videotape examples of skills/behaviors to be taught

       __21__ instructional games

       __8__ posters

       __4__ cue cards

       _____ other, please specify

8. Behavior management techniques for use during the teaching process and following integration

    __24__ praise   __16__ rewards

    __3__ warnings, reprimands   __13__ ignoring

    __18__ verbal instructions   __18__ mild punishment (denial of privileges, timeout)

    __21__ feedback   _____ other

9. Types of rewards preferred

    a. __4__ rewards at school only   a. __5__ freetime rewards only   a. __2__ group rewards only

    b. _____ rewards at home only   b. __1__ tangible rewards only   b. _____ individual rewards only

    c. __18__ both   c. __16__ both   c. __19__ both

    d. _____ neither   d. _____ neither   d. _____ neither

10. Record keeping

    a. __14__ forms for recording child progress

    b. __13__ graphs for charting progress

    c. __16__ behavioral observation forms/procedures

    d. __21__ behavior checklists of skills/competencies mastered

11. Technical assistance needs in preparing children for mainstreaming and in managing the integration process

    a. _____ none

    b. __21__ access to a teacher consultant

    c. __19__ parent involvement

    d. __9__ direct support from an IEP case manager

    e. __13__ provision of a teacher aide

    f. __17__ specific procedures of the type involved in the ACCEPTS instruments and instructional package

APPENDIX 4

Name _____ Position _____

ACCEPTS Program

Consumer Satisfaction Ratings of the ACCEPTS Curriculum and Behavior Management System

Instructions: The developers of the ACCEPTS Curriculum and accompanying behavior management system would appreciate your feedback as a potential or past user of these materials. Please respond to the questions below. Thank you.

ACCEPTS Curriculum

1. Does the ACCEPTS Curriculum teach skills that will positively affect the social and educational development of handicapped children?

    Social Development   *Educational Development*

    _____Yes   _____Yes

    _____No   _____No

    _____Unsure   _____Unsure

2. Please rate the overall appropriateness of the following:

    The curriculum content for teaching the above skills

    Not Appropriate   Moderately Appropriate   Highly Appropriate
    1............2............3............4............5............6............7

    The teaching formats

    Not Appropriate   Moderately Appropriate   Highly Appropriate
    1............2............3............4............5............6............7

The instructional procedures

Not Appropriate	Moderately Appropriate	Highly Appropriate
1............2............3............4............5............6............7		

The correction procedures

Not Appropriate	Moderately Appropriate	Highly Appropriate
1............2............3............4............5............6............7		

3. Are the guidelines for using the curriculum and instructional procedures sufficiently clear?

   _____Yes

   _____No

4. Is the introductory material in Section I useful?

   _____Yes

   _____No

   _____Unsure

5. How well organized is the curriculum?

   Not Well Organized   *Moderately Well Organized*   *Very Well Organized*
   1............2............3............4............5............6............7

6. Is the curriculum clearly written and understandable?

   _____Yes

   _____No

   _____Unsure

7. How effective do you think the curriculum is in teaching children essential behavioral and social skills?

   Handicapped Children

Not Effective	Moderately Effective	Highly Effective
1............2............3............4............5............6............7		

   Nonhandicapped Children

Not Effective	Moderately Effective	Highly Effective
1............2............3............4............5............6............7		

Behavior Management Procedures

1. Do you think the ACCEPTS behavior management procedures are an important part of the overall curriculum package?

    _____Yes

    _____No

    _____Unsure

2. How effective are they in strengthening previously taught curriculum skills?

    Not Effective   Moderately Effective   Highly Effective
    1............2............3............4............5............6............7

3. Are the procedures reasonably easy to use?

    _____Yes

    _____No

    _____Unsure

    Have you used the ACCEPTS Curriculum package to teach behavioral and social skills to either handicapped or nonhandicapped children?

    _____Yes

    _____No

    If yes, to how many children?

    _____Number of handicapped

    _____Number of nonhandicapped

Suggestions
If you have suggestions for improvement of the ACCEPTS Curriculum and behavior management system, please list them in the space below.

APPENDIX 5

SUMMARY: CONSUMER SATISFACTION RATINGS OF 157 SCHOOL PROFESSIONALS TRAINED IN HOW TO USE THE ACCEPTS PROGRAM

Consumer Satisfaction Items (See Appendix 4 For Item Descriptions)	ACCEPTS Program Users (N = 15)	ACCEPTS Program Workshop Participants (N = 142)		
ACCEPTS Curriculum		Consultants	Administrators	Teachers
Item Number				

1. a. Social Development
    1. ___Yes 2. ___No
    3. ___Unsure
	1. 100% 2. --- 3. ---	1. 100%
		2. ---
		3. ---
			1. 100%
			2. ---
			3. ---
				1. 97%
				2. ---
				3. 3%

b. Educational Development
    1. ___Yes 2. ___No
    3. ___Unsure
	1. 87% 2. --- 3. 13%	1. 76%
		2. ---
		3. 24%
			1. 100%
			2. ---
			3. ---
				1. 88%
				2. ---
				3. 12%

2. Likert Rating 1-7				
The curriculum content for teaching the above skills	$x = 6.47$ S.D. = .52	$x = 5.87$ S.D. = .68	$x = 6.71$ S.D. = .48	$x = 6.06$ S.D. = .75
The teaching formats	$x = 6.36$ S.D. = .84	$x = 5.82$ S.D. = .77	$x = 6.57$ S.D. = .53	$x = 5.85$ S.D. = .91
The instructional procedures	$x = 6.21$ S.D. = .80	$x = 5.72$ S.D. = .84	$x = 6.27$ S.D. = .49	$x = 5.97$ S.D. = .81
The correction procedures	$x = 6.02$ S.D. = .87	$x = 5.66$ S.D. = .94	$x = 6.00$ S.D. = .82	$x = 5.97$ S.D. = .81
3. Are the guidelines for using the curriculum and instructional procedures sufficiently clear?	100% Yes ___ No	100% Yes ___ No	100% Yes ___ No	100% Yes ___ No
4. Is the instructional materials in Section I useful?	86% Yes ___ No 14% Unsure	93% Yes ___ No 7% Unsure	86% Yes ___ No 14% Unsure	91% Yes ___ No 9% Unsure
Likert Rating 1-7				
5 How well organized is the curriculum?	$x = 6.4$ S.D. = .83	$x = 5.82$ S.D. = .95	$x = 6.5$ S.D. = .55	$x = 6.26$ S.D. = .82
6 Is the curriculum clearly written and understandable?	100% Yes ___ No ___ Unsure	93% Yes ___ No 7% Unsure	86% Yes ___ No 14% Unsure	99% Yes ___ No 1% Unsure
Likert Rating 1-7				

Consumer Satisfaction Items (See Appendix 4 For Item Descriptions) ACCEPTS Curriculum	ACCEPTS Program Users (N = 15)	ACCEPTS Program Workshop Participants (N = 142)		
		Consultants	Administrators	Teachers
Item Number				
7. How effective do you think the curriculum is in teaching children essential behavioral and social skills?				
Handicapped Children	x = 6.43 S.D. = .65	x = 5.41 S.D. = .82	x = 6.29 S.D. = .76	x = 6.04 S.D. = 1.00
Nonhandicapped Children	x = 5.44 S.D. = 1.01	x = 5.78 S.D. = .85	x = 5.71 S.D. = 1.11	x = 6.13 S.D. = .90
ACCEPTS Curriculum				
Behavior Management Procedures				
1. Do you think the ACCEPTS behavior management procedures are an important part of the overall curriculum package?	79% Yes 7% No 14% Unsure	97% Yes ___ No 3% Unsure	100% Yes ___ No ___ Unsure	94% Yes ___ No 6% Unsure
Likert Rating 1-7				
2. How effective are they in strengthening previously taught curriculum skills?	x = 6.4 S.D. = .84	x = 5.48 S.D. = .92	x = 5.71 S.D. = 1.11	x = 5.92 S.D. = .93
3. Are the procedures reasonably easy to use?	100% Yes ___ No ___ Unsure	86% Yes 3% No 11% Unsure	86% Yes ___ No 14% Unsure	96% Yes ___ No 4% Unsure
Have you used the ACCEPTS curriculum package to teach behavioral and social skills to either handicapped or nonhandicapped children?	100% Yes ___ No	___ Yes ___ No	___ Yes 100% No	___ Yes ___ No
If yes, to how many children?	x = 4.15 S.D. = 4.04			

APPENDIX 6

ACCEPTS SCREENING CHECKLIST

Rater Instructions. The items below describing classroom and peer-to-peer social behavior are designed for use in selecting target children who can benefit from the ACCEPTS program. You are asked to rate the child's behavior *in the setting* in which you are responsible for her or him.

In rating the child's *classroom behavior*, please use your *own* behavioral-academic expectations as a standard for making a *"yes"*, *"no"*, or *"unsure"* judgment. For example, if the child *does not* satisfactorily comply with your commands, you would check *"yes"* to Item 4 below. If he/she does comply satisfactorily, you would check *"no"*. If you cannot decide, check *"unsure"*.

In rating the child's social behavior, e.g., behavior directed toward peers, please rate the child's performance in relation to normal peers. For example, if the child usually *initiates less* to others than do normal peers, you would answer "yes" to Item 1 below. If as much or more, check "no", and if you can't decide, check "unsure".

Section I. Classroom Behavior

1. Does the child *fail to listen* to instructions and directions? ____Yes ____No ____Unsure
2. Does the child *fail to produce* work of acceptable quality? ____Yes ____No ____Unsure
3. Does the child *violate classroom rules*? ____Yes ____No ____Unsure
4. Is the child *noncompliant* to the instructions and directions of adults? ____Yes ____No ____Unsure

Section II. Social Behavior

1. Does the child *initiate* interactions *less often* than peers? ____Yes ____No ____Unsure
2. Does the child *talk less* than peers? ____Yes ____No ____Unsure
3. Does the child *fail to respond* to peers' initiations? ____Yes ____No ____Unsure
4. Is the child *more physically* or *verbally aggressive* than peers? ____Yes ____No ____Unsure
5. Do peers *ignore* the child? ____Yes ____No ____Unsure
6. Is the child *teased or picked on* more than peers? ____Yes ____No ____Unsure
7. Do peers *complain about* or *exclude* the child? ____Yes ____No ____Unsure
8. Is the child *hostile* or *antisocial* with others? ____Yes ____No ____Unsure

APPENDIX 7

THE ACCEPTS OBSERVATION FORM

The ACCEPTS Observation Form consists of two parts: (1) Instructions for recording classroom and peer-to-peer behavior, and (2) a record form for tallying the results of observation. Information produced by the form will allow you to directly evaluate the adequacy of the target child's classroom and playground adjustments. To record child behavior you will need a stopwatch with a stop/start switch and an ability to accumulate time and a standard definition for behavior in classroom and playground settings. Instructions for recording first classroom and then playground behavior are presented below.

Recording Classroom Behavior

The four items in Section I of the ACCEPTS Checklist are used as a standard for recording the child's classroom behavior. The great majority of teachers see these behaviors as incompatible with a satisfactory classroom adjustment.

In recording classroom behavior, note the time you begin observing and let the stopwatch run whenever the child engages in one or more of these inappropriate behaviors; that is, when the child is *not* behaving appropriately. Whenever the child's classroom behavior is appropriate, stop the stopwatch and leave it off until it again becomes inappropriate. At the end of the observation period, note the end time and calculate the total number of minutes you observed, divide this figure into the number of minutes on the stopwatch, and multiply the resulting figure by 100. This gives you the percent of time the child's behavior was inappropriate during the observation. For example, if you observed for a 20 minute period and had three minutes on the stopwatch, the "percent inappropriate" figure would be $3 \div 20 = .15 \times 100 = 15\%$. Enter this figure along with the date and the type of classroom activity (reading, math, language arts) in Section I of the ACCEPTS Recording Form.

Recording Playground Behavior

In freeplay or playground situations, social participation usually takes one of two forms: *spontaneous play* or *structured activities*. Handicapped and socially unskilled children tend to spend less time in spontaneous play and are often excluded from structured games and activities in these settings. The ACCEPTS Observation Form allows you to determine the degree of the referred or target child's participation with peers.

As with classroom behavior, a standardized definition of social behavior is necessary for recording. The definition used by the ACCEPTS developers is as follows:

Definition of Peer-to-Peer Social Behavior. An *active* exchange of social signals between two or more children that may involve verbal interaction, physical contact, active gesturing, playing catch, participating in a structured game or activity, or playing on playground equipment.

In recording, you should follow the steps below in sequence:

Step One.
Note the beginning and ending time of the recess period you observe in.

Step Two.
Using the above definition, let the stopwatch run whenever the child is socially participating and stop it whenever he/she is not participating.

Step Three.
Calculate the percent of time spent in social participation (e.g., percent social) by dividing the length (in minutes) of the recess period, or the total number of minutes you observed, into the number of minutes on the stopwatch. Multiply the resulting figure by 100 to obtain the percent social estimate. For example, if the target child socially participated for 21 minutes of a 30 minute recess period, the percent social figure would be $21 \div 30 = .70 \times 100 = 70\%$. Enter this figure along with the date in Section II of the ACCEPTS Recording Form. Also, check whether the recess was a.m., noon, or p.m.

Follow the guidelines below in making your observations.

Recording Guidelines. Sometimes it may be difficult to tell whether a child is actually interacting with someone else or simply engaging in parallel play. The key is whether the target child and her/his interactive partner(s) are orienting toward each other and exchanging social signals. If they are, the stopwatch is allowed to run, if not, it is shut off until a social exchange begins. Use the following rules to guide your coding.

(1) If there is a five second or more break in the exchange of social signals, shut off the stopwatch and leave it off until another social exchange begins.
(2) If a child is simply standing near or beside other children, but not interacting with them, *do not* run the stopwatch.
(3) If the child is engaged in a structured activity or game, let the watch run for as long as he or she is involved in the game, even though the child might not be interacting with anyone specifically during the activity.
(4) If the child is having a casual conversation with another child, let the watch run for as long as it lasts (remember to stop the watch if there is a five second or greater break in the social exchange).
(5) Record *all* the child's social behavior, even though portions of it may be negative or aggressive.

ACCEPTS RECORDING FORM

This form is used for tallying results of classroom and playground observations. Section I is for classroom observations and Section II for playground observations.

Section I

Observation Number _____   _____   _____

Observation Date _____/____/_____   _____/____/_____   _____/____/_____

Type of Classroom Activity _____   _____   _____

Percent Inappropriate _____   _____   _____

Section II

Observation Number _____   _____   _____

Observation Date _____/____/_____   _____/____/_____   _____/____/_____

Time of Recess am   noon   pm   am   noon   pm   am   noon   pm

Percent Social _____   _____   _____

APPENDIX 8

ACCEPTS PLACEMENT TEST

Teacher Rating Instructions

Please read each statement on the placement test carefully and circle the corresponding number that is descriptive/representative of the child's behavior. The numbers 1-5 are a *continuous* scale. Circling number 1 indicates that the statement is *not* descriptive or true; circling number 3 states that the statement is *moderately* descriptive or true of the child, and circling number 5 indicates it is *very* descriptive or true of the child.

For example, an item might read as follows:

The student shares laughter with classmates

Not descriptive or true	Moderately descriptive or true	Very descriptive or true
1..............2..............3..............4..............5		

If you feel the child does *not* share laughter with classmates, then by circling number 1 you would indicate that the statement is not descriptive or true of that child.

If you feel that the child does this *some* of the time, then by circling number 3 you would indicate that the statement is *moderately* descriptive or true.

If you feel that this happens most of the time, then by circling number 5 you would indicate that the statement is *very* descriptive or true of the child. Otherwise, circle the number (2 or 4) that most closely indicates your rating of the item.

Area I: Classroom Skills

	Not descriptive or true	Moderately descriptive or true	Very descriptive or true
1. The student sits quietly and pays attention to what the teacher is saying.	1..........2..........3..........4..........5		
2. When the teacher tells the student to do something, the student does it.	1..........2..........3..........4..........5		

	Not descriptive or true	Moderately descriptive or true	Very descriptive or true

3. The student produces work of acceptable quality.
1..........2..........3..........4..........5

4. The student follows the established classroom rules.
1..........2..........3..........4..........5

Area II: Basic Interaction Skills

1. The student maintains eye contact while speaking or when spoken to.
1..........2..........3..........4..........5

2. The student speaks in a moderate tone of voice (neither too loud/too soft).
1..........2..........3..........4..........5

3. The student seeks out others to interact with and initiates a conversation.
1..........2..........3..........4..........5

4. The student pays attention when spoken to.
1..........2..........3..........4..........5

5. The student responds/answers when spoken to.
1..........2..........3..........4..........5

6. The student converses by saying things which are relevant to the topic.
1..........2..........3..........4..........5

7. The student shares a conversation by speaking for about the same amount of time as they listen.
1..........2..........3..........4..........5

8. The student asks questions that request information about someone/something.
1..........2..........3..........4..........5

9. The student keeps a conversation going.
1..........2..........3..........4..........5

Area III: Getting Along Skills

1. The student uses polite words such as "please," "thank you," and "excuse me."
1..........2..........3..........4..........5

	Not descriptive or true	Moderately descriptive or true	Very descriptive or true

2. The student allows others to use or borrow something that belongs to them.　　1 . . . . 2 . . . . 3 . . . . 4 5

3. The student follows the rules when playing games with others.　　1 . . . . 2 . . . . 3 . . . . 4 5

4. The student takes initiative to assist others when they need help.　　1 . . . . 2 . . . . 3 . . . . 4 5

5. The student uses physical contact with others in an acceptable manner.　　1 . . . . 2 . . . . 3 . . . . 4 5

Area IV: Making Friends Skills

1. The student is clean and dresses neatly.　　1 . . . . 2 . . . . 3 . . . . 4 5

2. The student shows he/she likes something by smiling.　　1 . . . . 2 . . . . 3 . . . . 4 5

3. The student compliments by telling someone when he/she likes something.　　1 . . . . 2 . . . . 3 . . . . 4 5

4. .The student initiates making friends by: seeking out others to interact with, initating conversation, taking turns talking, and asking the person to spend time with her/him.　　1 . . . . 2 . . . . 3 . . . . 4 5

Area V: Coping Skills

1. The student finds other ways to play when he/she asks to join an activity and the answer is, "no."　　1 . . . . 2 . . . . 3 . . . . 4 5

2. The student expresses anger by telling someone he/she is angry without hurting them.　　1 . . . . 2 . . . . 3 . . . . 4 5

3 When someone teases the student, he/she looks away and does not answer.　　1 . . . . 2 . . . . 3 . . . . 4 5

	Not descriptive or true	Moderately descriptive or true	Very descriptive or true
4. When someone tries to hurt/fight with the student, he/she tries to walk away.	1..........2	3	..........4..........5
5. When someone asks the student to do something he/she cannot do, or does not want to do, the student says, "no" politely.	1..........2	3	..........4..........5
6. When things are not going well, the student tries another way.	1..........2	3	..........4..........5

APPENDIX 9

ACCEPTS Placement Test

SUMMARY SHEET

Each item on the Placement Test has an assigned *Area*, a *Number*, and an ACCEPTS skill which corresponds to it.

1. Fill in your rating for each item under the column which says *RATING*.
2. Place a checkmark beside those items given a rating of 1, 2, or 3.
3. For those items checkmarked, it is strongly recommended that the teacher teach the corresponding ACCEPTS SKILL(S) referred to in the right hand column.

AREA	NUMBER	RATING	SKILL
I. CLASSROOM SKILLS:	1	_____	Listening to the teacher
	2	_____	When the teacher tells you to do something
	3	_____	Doing your best work
	4	_____	Following the classroom rules
II. BASIC INTERACTION SKILLS:	1	_____	Eye contact
	2	_____	Using the right voice
	3	_____	Starting
	4	_____	Listening
	5	_____	Answering
	6	_____	Making sense
	7	_____	Taking turns talking

AREA	NUMBER	RATING	SKILL
	8	_____	A question
	9	_____	Continuing
III. GETTING ALONG: SKILLS	1	_____	Using polite words
	2	_____	Sharing
	3	_____	Following the rules
	4	_____	Assisting others
	5	_____	Touching the right way
IV. MAKING FRIENDS: SKILLS	1	_____	Grooming
	2	_____	Smiling
	3	_____	Complimenting
	4	_____	Making friends
V. COPING SKILLS:	1	_____	When someone says "no"
	2	_____	Expressing anger
	3	_____	When someone teases you
	4	_____	When someone tries to hurt you
	5	_____	When someone asks you to do something you can't do
	6	_____	When things don't go right

APPENDIX 10

DESCRIPTIONS OF THE ACCEPTS VIDEO SCENES FOR USE IN MODELING POSITIVE AND NEGATIVE EXAMPLES

The material below is provided for your use if you do not have access to the ACCEPTS videotape. A brief description of each scene in the videotape is presented for your convenience.

You, as the teacher, can model the scenes or a skilled group of students can act out the scenes under your supervision. The latter option is usually preferable because so many of the scenes involve peer interaction.

AREA I: CLASSROOM SKILLS

Skill #1: Listening to the Teacher

First *positive* example: Teacher gives instructions to the class. The students sit quietly, listen, and look at the teacher while she speaks.

Negative example: Seth makes a paper airplane and Melissa plays with her pencil while the teacher is giving instructions.

Second *positive* example: The entire class is listening and following the instructions the teacher is giving.

Skill #2: When the Teacher Tells You to Do Something

First *positive* example: Ryan spills a glass of water and follows the teacher's instructions when she asks him to clean it up.

Negative example: Mark leaves his seat without permission. The teacher reminds him to follow the classroom rule of asking permission to leave his seat.

Second *positive* example: The teacher tells Melissa to stop disturbing another student and get back to work. She does what the teacher asks.

Other *positive* examples:
1. The teacher calls a student to her desk to review his work and praises him for quickly doing what she asked.
2. Seth is asked to help straighten up the classroom and is praised by the teacher for doing so.
3. When the principal visits the class and asks Heidi to clean up some papers, she does what he asks.

Skill #3: Doing Your Best Work

First *positive* example: The teacher praises Mark for using his best handwriting and following directions on an assignment.

Negative example: Melissa is told she hasn't done her work neatly and must copy it over before getting freetime.

Second *positive* example: A student is praised for doing her work neatly, and allowed to go to freetime.

AREA II: BASIC INTERACTION SKILLS

Skill #2: Using the Right Voice

First *positive* example: Three girls are making

plans for their state project using normal tones of voice while talking.

Negative example: The same girls are making plans and one of them yells that she has an idea! The other two girls tell her not to talk so loudly.

Skill #3: Starting

First *positive* example: A girl initiates a game of hopscotch with a boy.

Negative example: Seth is playing blocks alone, wishing he had someone to play with, but he doesn't ask the boy sitting next to him to play with him.

Second *positive* example: This time Seth asks Mark to play with him.

Other *positive* examples:
1. A student suggests to another that they take turns pushing each other on the swing.
2. A girl asks another girl if she would like to help her with a puzzle.
3. A boy asks if he can join other students in a game of dodge-ball.

Skill #4: Listening

First *positive* example: Danny listens to a friend tell about his new pen.

Negative example: While one girl is talking, another hums to herself and plays with her fingers. The first girl leaves to play with someone else.

Second *positive* example: When Melissa's friend talks about her new pants, Melissa listens and responds.

Third *positive* example: Danny listens and responds to a friend talking about his bike.

Skill #5: Answering

First *positive* example: When a boy is asked to look at the pictures two girls have drawn, he stops to listen, look, and answer.

Negative example: This time he ignores them and leaves when he is asked to look at the pictures.

Second *positive* example: Two students cooperate to draw a picture after one student asks the other if they'd like to help draw.

Other *positive* examples:
1. A student asks a boy playing with her if he can hang upside down. He answers that he can, and shows her, then they continue playing.
2. Two boys ask another boy to play kickball with them.

Skill #6: Making Sense

First *positive* example: Two girls discuss their spelling assignment—they are both talking about the same thing.

Negative example: When one boy talks about a funny t.v. show he watched the night before, Danny talks about his Dad's new car.

Second *positive* example: This time Danny talks about the t.v. show, too. Both boys are talking about the same thing.

Skill #7: Taking Turns Talking

First *positive* example: Two girls discuss a party one of them is going to have.

Negative example: When a boy tries to talk to Danny, he talks, but doesn't let Danny talk.

Second *positive* example: Two girls discuss a friend's new outfit.

Other *positive* examples:
1. Two boys discuss a friend's new outfit.
2. Two girls have a conversation about cats.
3. A boy and girl discuss a drawing they're going to make.

Skill #8: A Question

First *positive* example: A girl asks a boy in her class if he likes to play cards and what his favorite game is, then asks him to play cards with her.

Second *positive* example: Two girls talk with each other about their favorite cookies, asking each other what their favorite cookies are. They agree to get together to bake cookies.

Third *positive* example: Two girls talk together and ask each other questions about their favorite t.v. shows and sports.

Skill -9: Continuing

First *positive* example: Two boys talk about going to the fair, and the rides they went on, then decide to play catch.

Second *positive* example: A girl asks another student if she can help her with a puzzle. While working on the puzzle they talk about a field trip to the airport, then decide to go outside and play.

AREA III: GETTING ALONG SKILLS

Skill #2: Sharing

First *positive* example: When a classmate asks Seth if Seth will loan her his scissors, he readily agrees and gives her the scissors.
Negative example: This time when she asks Seth to share his scissors, he says no and they begin to argue. The teacher intervenes and takes away their freetime.
Other *positive* examples:
1. A boy and girl share markers for drawing.
2. Two girls want to buy gum after school, but don't have enough money individually. One girl suggests they put their money together to buy gum to share.

Skill #3: Following Rules

First *positive* example: A boy and girl are playing checkers together. When the girl says she needs to be "kinged", the boy "kings" her, then takes his turn.
Negative example: Ricardo refuses to be "it" in a game of tag and a playmate yells that he is ruining the game.
Second *positive* example: This time Ricardo agrees to be "it" and the game continues.
Other *positive* examples:
1. A girl makes a wrong move playing checkers and her classmate corrects her.
2. Three students playing foursquare ask a fourth student to join the game. When he says he doesn't know the rules, one of the students explains them to him.

Skill #4: Assisting Others

First *positive* example: Dee Dee asks a classmate if she can help her move a table.
Negative example: The girl tries to move the table alone, but Dee Dee ignores her and doesn't help.
Other *positive* examples:
1. Dee Dee helps a classmate on the balance beam.
2. Danny helps Dee Dee with a paper project.
3. A boy helps a classmate put a project together.

AREA IV: MAKING FRIENDS SKILLS

Skill #1: Good Grooming

First *positive* example: A girl tells a classmate that she looks nice.
Negative example: Heidi's classmate tells her that no one plays with her because she looks messy.

Skill #2: Smiling

First *positive* example: A girl reads a story to Dee Dee, who smiles and says she likes it.
Negative example: This time when she reads the story to Dee Dee, Dee Dee doesn't smile, which makes her friend angry.

Skill #3: Complimenting

First *positive* example: A boy tells a classmate he likes her running shoes.
Negative example: While playing together, a girl thanks her classmate for letting her be his partner during stretching exercises that day.
Other *positive* examples:
1. A boy compliments another boy on his kick.
2. A boy tells his classmate she makes nice pictures and that he wishes he could make pictures like that.
3. When two classmates help a boy move a table, he thanks them.

Skill #4: Making Friends

First *positive* example: Melissa and Dee Dee exchange names, information about where each other lives, and then decide to play together after school.

Second *positive* example: A girl tells a friend she thinks he's really good at doing flips and asks where he learned. He tells her he learned in a class and invites her to come to the class someday.

AREA V: COPING SKILLS

Skill #1: When Someone Says "No"

First *positive* example: A girl asks if she can join a group of girls playing jumprope, but is told they already have enough people. She says she'll get another jumprope so they can all play.

Negative example: A girl asks to play the winner at checkers. When she's told they're playing a tournament and the winner has to play two out of three games, she says they're hogging the game and goes to tell the teacher.

Second *positive* example: When a girl is told she can't join a game of "Fish" two other girls are playing, she decides to play another game.

Other *positive* examples:
1. A girl asks two classmates if she can play with them and one of them says she doesn't like her and tells her to leave. The girl leaves and finds someone else to play with.
2. A girl wants to help two classmates draw, but is told there aren't anymore markers. She says she has crayons and gets them so they can all use them.

Skill #2: When You Express Anger

First *positive* example: Mark knocks a box of crayons off Seth's desk. Seth tells him it wasn't a nice thing to do; that Mark did it on purpose and he doesn't like it.

Negative example: Mark and Seth are playing catch and Seth accidentally hits Mark with the ball. Mark gets upset, yells and pushes Seth, and refuses to play anymore.

Second *positive* example: When Mark gets hit this time, he tells Seth it hurt, but that since it was an accident it's O.K.

Other *positive* examples:
1. When Dee Dee tries to disturb Melissa while she's working, Melissa tells her to leave her alone; she has work to do and will talk to her at recess.
2. When Seth takes a toy away from Mark and shoves him, Mark expresses his anger to Seth, but doesn't hit him back.

Skill #3: When Someone Teases You

First *positive* example: When a classmate teases him about being slow in math, Danny refuses to respond and talks to another student.

Negative example: A girl teases a classmate by calling him names and shoving him. He responds by telling her to shut up and shoving her back.

Other *positive* examples:
1. Danny calls Mark names and Mark gets up and walks away from him.
2. Melissa teases Heidi about her clothes, but Heidi responds by ignoring her and changing the subject.
3. Danny teases a classmate, who ignores him and continues playing with her friend.

Skill #4: When Someone Tries to Hurt You

First *positive* example: When a girl bullies another girl, the girl bullied tells her to leave her alone, then walks away.

Other *positive* examples:
1. Two girls are playing checkers and the loser accuses the winner of cheating, then dumps the checkers onto the table and walks off. The other girl raises her hand and calls for the teacher.
2. Instead of fighting back, a boy walks away from a classmate after he starts to roughhouse with him.
3. When two boys play too rough together and one is thrown to the ground, his friend apologizes for being so rough and helps him up.

Skill #5: When Someone Asks You to Do Something You Can't Do

First *positive* example: Dee Dee doesn't get upset when her friend politely tells her she can't use a blue crayon because she's using it.

Negative example: Dee Dee rudely tells her friend she can't play when her friend asks her to play flashcards with her.

Second *positive* example: This time Dee Dee politely explains to her friend why she can't play flashcards with her.

Other *positive* examples:

1. A girl politely explains to her classmate why she can't help her with a word puzzle.
2. Dee Dee's friend doesn't get upset when Dee Dee politely tells her she doesn't feel like playing.
3. When Dee Dee asks for help with a film projector, her two classmates explain they can't help, but offer to help if she doesn't find anyone else to help.

APPENDIX 11

Sample Praise Statements

1. You're doing a good job!
2. You did a lot of work today!
3. Now you've figured it out.
4. That's RIGHT!!!
5. Now you've got the hang of it.
6. That's the way!
7. You're really going to town!
8. You're doing fine!
9. Now you have it!
10. Nice going
11. That's great!
12. You did it that time!
13. GREAT!
14. FANTASTIC!
15. TERRIFIC!
16. Good for you!
17. GOOD WORK!
18. That's better.
19. EXCELLENT!
20. Good job, (name of student).
21. You outdid yourself today!
22. That's the best you've ever done
23. Good going!
24. Keep it up!
25. That's really nice
26. WOW!
27. Keep up the good work.
28. Much better!
29. Good for you!
30. That's very much better.
31. Good thinking!
32. Exactly right!
33. SUPER!
34. Nice going.
35. You make it look easy
36. Way to go!
37. Superb!
38. You're getting better every day.
39. WONDERFUL!
40. I knew you could do it.
41. Keep working on it, you're getting better.
42. You're doing beautifully.
43. You're really working hard today.
44. That's the way to do it!
45. Keep on trying!
46. THAT'S it!
47. You've got it made.
48. You're very good at that.
49. You're learning fast.
50. I'm very proud of you.
51. You certainly did well today.
52. That's good.
53. I'm happy to see you working like that.
54. I'm proud of the way you worked today.
55. That's the right way to do it.
56. You're really learning a lot.
57. That's better than ever.
58. That's quite an improvement.
59. That kind of work makes me very happy.
60. Now you've figured it out.
61. PERFECT!
62. FINE!
63. That's IT!
64. You figured that out fast.
65. You remembered!
66. You're really improving.
67. I think you've got it now.
68. Well look at you go!
69. TREMENDOUS!
70. OUTSTANDING!
71. Now that's what I call a fine job.
72. You did that very well.
73. That was first class work.
74. Right on!
75. SENSATIONAL!
76. That's the best ever.
77. Good remembering!
78. You haven't missed a thing.
79. You really make my job fun.
80. You must have been practicing.

Appendix 12

POINTS RECORDING FORM

THINGS TO DO (That earn Points)   M   T   W   TH   F

TOTALS   ____ ____ ____ ____ ____

THINGS NOT TO DO (That lose Points)

TOTALS   ____ ____ ____ ____ ____

APPENDIX 13

ACCEPTS RECESS RATING FORM

Child's Name _____ Date _____

Rater's Name _____

General Instructions. The target child's *social participation* and *social skill level* is rated in a single daily recess period. A new form should be used for each daily rating. Specific instructions for making these ratings and for using the form are provided below.

Social Participation

Rater: The child's social participation is evaluated and rated in 5-minute segments throughout the recess period. "YES" is circled if the child has interacted appropriately for *at least half of the 5-minute period.* Appropriate interaction includes (a) active involvement in a game, (b) participation in an organized playground activity, or (c) talking to peers. "NO" is circled if the child does not interact with peers for more than half of the 5-minute period *or* the child engages in negative/inappropriate interactions for at least half of the period. Negative/inappropriate interaction includes such behaviors as arguing, teasing, hitting, and obstructing games.

To the child: Before recess, review with the child:

A. Things to do to *earn* freetime

    1. Play with friends (monkey bars, sandbox, foursquare, etc.).
    2. Play games (baseball, dodgeball, Red Rover, etc.).
    3. Talk to friends.

B. Things that *don't earn* freetime

    1. Being alone.
    2. Watching games, but not playing.
    3. Arguing with or teasing other children.
    4. Hurting people.

Rating

Recess Period   **Points Earned**

Recess Period	Points Earned	
1st 5-minute period	YES	NO
2nd 5-minute period	YES	NO
3rd 5-minute period	YES	NO
4th 5-minute period	YES	NO
5th 5-minute period	YES	NO
6th 5-minute period	YES	NO

½ minute of freetime is earned for each YES circled.

TOTAL freetime earned for playing with friends   _____

Skill Level Rating and Review

Rater: At the end of each recess period, the target child is evaluated and rated on the use of specific social skills taught in the ACCEPTS curriculum. This rating focuses on the use of a smaller number (3) of social skills. As these may be difficult for the child or newly learned, it is important that he/she be rewarded for using them. When you see the child engaging in one of the skills listed below, provide brief verbal praise. At the end of the recess period, indicate skills used by circling "YES" on the appropriate line. If the skill was not exhibited, circle "NO"

Skills to Focus On

1. _____ YES   NO

2. _____ YES   NO

3. _____ YES   NO

Review with the child the "Skills to Focus On" before recess. Tell the child you will be watching especially for those skills, but you want to see other skills used appropriately also.

1 minute of freetime is earned for each YES circled

TOTAL freetime earned for Focus skills   _____

Also at the end of recess, the child's overall social skill level is evaluated and rated on a scale of 0 to 5 ("0" representing unskilled and "5" highly skilled). This rating should reflect the *degree* to which all social skills are displayed and the child's *skill level* in applying them.

Overall Skill Level

Unskilled   *Highly Skilled*
    1..............2..................3..................4..................5

1 minute of freetime is earned for each point on the scale

TOTAL freetime minutes earned for Overall Skill Level   _____

After recess spend a moment with the child to:
1. Ask questions about the activities completed and skills used. Prompt and praise the child for accurately describing their behavior during recess.
2. Debrief and provide feedback to the child, detailing (a) activities/skills you observed, (b) skills the child successfully applied, and (c) skills the child should have applied, or instances where skills were not properly used.
3. Explain the ratings you have recorded for the child. Whenever possible, praise the child for positive aspects of his/her performance.

APPENDIX 14

FORM FOR RECORDING AND TRACKING
EARNED CLASSROOM POINTS
AND FREETIME MINUTES AT RECESS

		Earned	Spent	Balance	Cumulative Total
	Classroom Points	_____	_____	_____	_____
_____	Freetime Minutes	_____	_____	_____	_____
	Classroom Points	_____	_____	_____	_____
_____	Freetime Minutes	_____	_____	_____	_____
	Classroom Points	_____	_____	_____	_____
_____	Freetime Minutes	_____	_____	_____	_____
	Classroom Points	_____	_____	_____	_____
_____	Freetime Minutes	_____	_____	_____	_____
	Classroom Points	_____	_____	_____	_____
_____	Freetime Minutes	_____	_____	_____	_____

APPENDIX 15

Classroom Behavior Daily Rating Form

Child's Name _____   Date _____

Teacher _____

Instructions: Please rate the appropriateness of the child's classroom behavior on a scale of 1 to 5 during designated academic periods.

Inappropriate   *Appropriate*
1................2................3................4................5

Please use the following list of appropriate classroom behaviors as criteria in making your rating:

(1) Listening to instructions and directions
(2) Making assistance needs known
(3) Producing work of acceptable quality.
(4) Following established classroom rule
(5) Complying with teacher instructions/commands

If the child complied with these criteria during the rating period, he/she should receive a high rating. If not, then a lower rating should be given. Explain the rating to the child and provide verbal praise for good performance. Write a brief comment about good performance when the child receives a rating of 3 or higher.

APPENDIX 16

ACCEPTS RECESS RATING FORM

Playground Supervisor's Version

Child's Name _____ Date _____

Supervisor's Name _____

General Instructions. Divide the recess period into four approximately equal segments. Evaluate the child's behavior at the end of each segment. If the child is involved in social participation, circle a "+" below; if not, circle a "−".

> Segment 1   +   −
>
> Segment 2   +   −
>
> Segment 3   +   −
>
> Segment 4   +   −

Also rate the child's overall skill level in displaying specific social skills while interacting with peers. Use the scale below.

Skill Level

Unskilled   Highly Skilled

1 . . . . 2 . . . . 3 . . . . 4 5

Praises

Circle the number of praises given during the recess period(s).

1   2   3   4   5   6   7   8   9   10